CREATE

YOUR OWN

DESTINY!

CREATE
YOUR OWN
DESTINY!

SPIRITUAL PATH TO SUCCESS

RACHEL MADORSKY

AVANTY HOUSE

Madorsky, Rachel.
    Create your own destiny! : spiritual path to success
/ Rachel Madorsky. – 1st ed
    p. cm.
    Includes bibliographical references and index.
    LCCN 2003092022
    ISBN 0-9705349-4-9

    1. Spiritual healing and spiritualism. 2. Success.
3. Self-realization. 4. Self-care, Health.   I. Title.

BF1275. F3M33 2003   615.8'52
                            QBI33-1343

Printed in the United States of America by Morris Publishing

*T*o my parents,

my first teachers,
and to my husband
and three sons,
my best friends

CONTENTS

ILLUSTRATIONS

POEMS

ACKNOWLEDGEMENTS

It is with deep appreciation that I thank those who have supported and helped me in the writing of this book as well as those who assisted in the preparation of the final manuscript. Included in this list are:

First, my husband, my first reader and critic. Second, those who edited and helped me to prepare the manuscript: Celia, Gail, Helen, Irene, James, Jerry, Joseph, Lee, Linda, Lynda, Randy, Peggy, Rich, Ron and "March." Third, but not least, my family and friends, who supported me throughout this long process and patients who pushed me to record their valuable experiences and outcomes. Special thanks to my son Nathaniel for sharing some of his poems.

People seldom realize that humanity's journey to knowledge aspires to one goal: to know oneself and one's soul and to know that part of the Universe that connects us with it. The unity of the spiritual and physical health of a human being can be attained through this search.

—R. Madorsky

FOREWORD

Create Your Own Destiny! is an important guidebook in identifying who is really the master of one's health, for good health is much more than taking a few pills when one becomes ill. Healing is a whole mind-set with spiritual implications and cosmic forces.

For centuries, cultures relied upon their high priests, medicine men, shamans, witch doctors, acupuncturists, or herbalists to cure disease. All these healers had a common bond – a belief in the power to heal. But the real underlying thread is that we – as patients – are guardians of our own good health and that healers are only catalysts in the process.

Identification of disease demands courage in the patient to reconsider spiritual and life values, and courage to face the truth. Once the disease has been identified, one of the first steps a patient learns is to know himself, for the real healing of the human body begins with the renewal of spirit. Meditation, visualization, and prayer also play roles in healing, along with diet and exercise.

This book explains that our bodies and minds are not two entities to be treated separately in the healing process but are woven into one. The body cannot banish a cancerous growth without first joining forces with the mind to provide a united front against the invading force. The path to healing is fiercely guarded and only those with spiritual maturity may pass. Those who do not change their inner selves cannot expect to make the journey.

Both healer and patient must work in concert to regain good health. This book was written at the request of the author's patients who felt that her voice needed to be heard and that her vision needed to be unveiled. As such, this book is truly a powerful channel to regaining one's health, for good health is not to be taken lightly. Good health must be held closely in the mind to preserve it.

Rachel is indeed an individual with unique gifts. Although there are healers on different planes, Rachel is a healer at the highest level. However, before an individual embarks on the journey to heal the body, the individual must undertake the spiritual quest to heal the soul.

Travel with Rachel Madorsky as she takes you on a healer's quest for knowledge and understanding of the Quasiworld and how it affects the physical body. Learn how choices made today may affect your physical well being. Deeper your spiritual understanding of the intangible realm that surrounds us – the invisible world.

Peggy Grillot, Past President,
Illinois Woman's Press Association

INTRODUCTION

Bioenergy healers are of two general kinds: those who are born and those who study with a training program such as Reiki or Bioenergy Therapy. Within both groups are persons who can produce interesting phenomena and healing effects. The trained groups show the stamp of the school where they learned their craft. The "naturals" are as varied as any group of human beings you will ever see. Their stories are different, their techniques are different, and their conceptualizations of what they do are different. One author, name long forgotten, speculated that a high-level intuitive was born with a frequency of about 1 in 43,000 births. I do not know if the number is correct, but I do know that my experience as an enthusiast for paranormal healing and a researcher of alternative therapies suggests that powerful healers of the "natural type" are very rare. Even more rare are natural healers with extensive education and any scientific background. Rachel Madorsky fills the description – natural healer, nurse, engineer, and college professor. She brings a background in both the physical and medical sciences, and in metaphysics to her work.

Create Your Own Destiny! Spiritual Path to Success is really two books in one. One is about a person with a gift for healing, raised in a family where this was considered a good thing and nurtured instead of punished, as it so often is in most situations. Accepting the gift with all the ramifications it brought to her – the struggle to develop a worldview that was both scientifically and metaphysically sound, the ethical choices, the conflict with typical medical care and paradigms and so on – are a part of the pages that follow. This is a woman of courage who set out to understand her healing gift and make it work better. She also needs to make her experiences available to others who are called to the healing path – for education, encouragement and understanding.

The second book is for persons with life-threatening diseases who are searching for answers. Scattered throughout the text are the startling conclusions Ms. Madorsky has reached about the metaphysical truths behind health and disease. She, along with many other mystics from ancient times, sees health and disease as only surface manifestations of a multifaceted life that has seen and unseen aspects that transcend time and space. She continually emphasizes the role of personal and family karma in our current health, particularly in the class of difficult diseases called cancer. This model places health as an outcome of physical, genetic, emotional, mental, spiritual and past life influences. Within the model she offers is also a powerful role for the individual human being, who has the responsibility to choose to understand the clues offered as to the true causes of health problems and to use that understanding to move toward health and healing. She indicates that even in the most extreme of life-threatening situations, spiritual forces are available to help fight for life and health if the individual is willing to accept the truth of his or her soul. We seem to choose our destiny more often than we usually are willing or able to admit.

For the person struggling to find answers to a health crisis, this book gives some places to look for understanding and a model for fitting together the answers. The experiences of others are offered as examples and options. The concepts are hard to grasp at first but are basically simple – all thoughts and actions have consequences, both immediately and on the subtle levels of reality that transcend a single lifetime. The energy of some acts carries over to both the future lifetimes of an individual soul and to genetic descendants over generations – the "sins of the fathers..." Thus one of the roots of dread diseases, particularly cancer, is the soul history and family lineage of the patient. One of the messages of the book is that even on this level, there is hope for different outcomes if one has the courage to choose to seek answers through exploration and intuition. Intuition is held as the final judge of truth as it applies to the individual seeker.

I frankly do not know if Rachel's conceptualizations and conclusions about how cancer works on a metaphysical level are "true" or not. They seem to work for her and her clients and, from a practical standpoint, that is what matters. Her debts to her studies of many philosophical and ancient healing traditions are evident as she outlines the use of hand reading, dreams and intuition as tools for finding connections and answers. She also draws on the insights provided by the non-physical teachers who guide her work, as well as her accumulated experience as a practitioner. The fundamental basis of her conclusions, however, remains her personal experiences and informal experiments. These are not totally idiosyncratic. Her ideas are congruent with other teachings – the American mystic Edgar Cayce, for example, as well as many other healers of the natural variety. Her work also seems to resonate with shamanic traditions from Asia, South America and the native people of North America. Perhaps some future scientists will unravel the mysteries of reincarnation, karma and the energy bodies that permeate the wisdom teaching of many cultures. Rachel offers some good clues as to where to look.

Overall, the book *Create Your Own Destiny! Spiritual Path to Success* gives a fascinating look into the mind and practices of a rare individual – a natural healer who has taken up the lonely task of understanding and using her gifts for the good of those who find their way to her practice. She does not claim to be able to heal any and all cases – her intuitive guidance sometimes advises her to say no to individuals in need. Not all seekers of health are willing to face the challenges that are involved in changing karma and not everyone will accept the model of health, disease, and reality she follows. Nonetheless, the book is a valuable one-of-a-kind look at a work in progress, the evolving knowledge and beliefs of a natural practitioner of an ancient healing tradition. Enjoy the trip. Be open and listen for that which speaks to you and your situation.

Jerry E. Wesch, Ph.D., President,
International Society for the Study of
Subtle Energies and Energy Medicine

The Truth

*S*pirit of the myth is rising,
Beyond the reach of comprehension
Belonging to the teaching.

Mastered knowledge is thought as bird
Above the ground and clouds,
In flight to heavens and the light.

Vanity untouched by virtues of truth.
Ignored its ascent to light
With vision of a peaceful future.

Equivalent to walls in structure,
The truth is noticed in a path.
Merely as walls the path is changed,
To go around.

Afraid of truth and possibilities of what might be,
Not coming close enough to take a peek
To satisfy the curiosity at hand.

Nathaniel Madorsky

There are two ways to live one's
life – as if nothing is a miracle
or as if everything is.
—Albert Eistein

Chapter 1

VISION
UNVEILED

*If we would have new knowledge, we must
get a whole world of new questions.*
—Susanne K. Langer

It is quite realistic to presume that by the time this book is published, new points of view, hypotheses and theories will have appeared to explain many of the scientific phenomena and facts mentioned in this book. Science and the human thirst for knowledge has no boundaries and will continue to advance on the foundation of our ancestors' labor.

This circumstance reminds me of the classical diagram in philosophy depicting our current knowledge concentrated inside a circle, while our ignorance is what lies beyond the circumference. The expanding volume of information inspires a perpetually growing aspiration to grasp the unknown. The more we know, the more we want to know. What reaches beyond the borders of the circumference of the known? The boundless uncertainty of the unknown, magnetically attracts generation after generation of scientists. From millennium to millennia, we attempt unceasingly to find answers to one big question: for what purpose do we exist in the human form in which we reproduce ourselves on Earth?

Destiny has bestowed on me the role of a healer. My inner-guide says, "This is your duty, from day to day, to cure people." As a result, I have accumulated and studied a good deal of evidence about the healing of the spiritual as well as the physical body and their fusion in the struggle for health, for the complete healing of the whole human organism.

We have to accept the wisdom of our ancestors transmitted to each of us through birth. We especially have to respect the truth that has been passed down to us through generations. We have to find the courage to refuse to accept at face value everything told to us by orthodox medical practitioners. Don't misunderstand! Physicians trained in modern medicine can benefit our lives. We should consider their knowledge, but not as though it was the ultimate or complete truth. Modern pharmaceutical medicine evolved approximately 100 years ago when aspirin tablets were introduced. Aspirin in its natural form, willow bark, has been prescribed during millennia by people who call themselves healers, shamans, priests, and medicine-men, or other names synonymous to the Latin word "doctor" – teacher, or practitioner of healing arts.

My book, based on real data and experience, will be equally useful to healthy people as well as to those who are intuitively aware that they are sick, but are afraid to accept this truth. Even those whose illness has progressed so far that they no longer believe in any cure for the affliction can learn something useful. The organic and functional transformations called diseases, once initiated, may be stopped or reversed at almost any point.

Much of my knowledge comes from my recent incarnation as well as previous ones. People of all races, nationalities, cultures and religions must recognize the value of accumulated experience. Every one of us has (his or her) own knowledge and understanding, which is priceless. I will share mine with you.

The inspiration for writing this book came from a conversation with a physician with whom I shared my impressions about the healing process in one of my earliest clients who was afflicted with terminal cancer. Despite the negative prognosis, the patient felt better and better after each of our sessions. On the advice of this physician, I began to compile and to analyze information on each patient I treated.

I believe that the information presented here will find its way even to those readers who, despite resistance, find the urge to aid sufferers through their own unusual gifts of healing. This book is not only for people who want to heal themselves, but also for people who may discover that they have healing abilities. Sometimes that discovery is met with resistance of their souls. I hope this book will enlighten those unique individuals who haven't yet accepted their destiny and are frightened by the healing gifts concealed in the deep recesses of their souls. Some information included in the book comes from lectures I have delivered to different organizations and from articles written for newspapers when numerous questions arose and I felt I should write about my personal experience.

Since ancient times humans have sought to unravel the mystery of their destiny on Earth. Much has been accomplished by individuals who have discovered personal spiritual missions in the material world. The underlying mystery of reality can be ignored but not avoided; it is independent of our will. Finding ways for its elucidation is alluring and part of my task.

Different sources, which have survived the centuries, bear witness to the invisible and often impalpable reality behind appearances. Engravings found on the walls of Pyrenean caves reflect the work of healers, as do descriptions in ancient Egyptian scrolls. The methods of treatment that act upon the energetic formations of organisms, as legends testify, were discovered in the East about 3000 B.C. In the Dead Sea scrolls, which were found in mountain caves located above an unearthed Qumran settlement in Israel belonging to the Essene sect, researchers discovered many world-shaking facts. The Essenes routinely trained members of their community in the practice of curing diseases by the laying on hands. A number of people in the Essenian sect demonstrated astonishing healing miracles by touching the afflicted with their hands. The cave sketches of American Indians depicting a treatment process with hand healing, practiced since ancient times on the Eurasian continent, testify to the permanence and universality of such treatment. Since then we haven't changed; the only thing that has changed is our approach to caring for our bodies.

The component material parts of the body and its functional physiology have been well investigated under the microscope and are sufficiently catalogued at this time. Modern medicine treats a human being as a mechanic does an automobile: let's fix it here and there, replacing one worn-out part for a new one. There is little comprehension of the human body as an entity. Medicine disregards the spiritual being of a person – the state of interconnection of the soul with the body.

Those seeking the truth about healing will find advice and recommendations in this book interwoven into the fabric of the stories about specific cases. The merit and value of techniques reside in their uniqueness as well as in how they are applied. They emphasize the importance of fortifying your spiritual condition in the struggle to recover good health and reveal the steps necessary to take, should the illness exceed permissible boundaries. Advice is presented on how to use the services of the untapped bioenergetic forces, a practice considered heresy in earlier times. Through modern technology, the hidden has become apparent, noted in science, and is a recognized phenomenon in the arsenal of the struggle for human health.

From my observation, viral and other infections are secondary events that often distort the understanding of the prime cause: the disruption of the interrelationships between our spiritual being and the laws of the Universe and its Creator.

In the text I have used only factual material about my patients, friends and acquaintances. There were some I knew before they were diagnosed either by me or through current medical methods; others came to me for consultation after receiving a tragic prognosis. Still others I observed from the sidelines, reluctant to disturb their peace. All names, initials, and in some cases the places have been changed.

As one former Lama said: "Why should you conduct experiments again and again and spend your precious time and material means, when everything is already described in the books written by Tibetan and other ancient sages in immemorial times? Only two conditions are necessary: to read and translate into the individual mind."

Many such books have been translated into the major languages, although they are interpreted differently, while others are still waiting for their time for the erudite philosopher and scientist to make them available. It is quite difficult not only to translate them, but also to read them. We have grown far apart from Nature and its knowledge. It is not easy to understand and translate what your parents and forefathers have distanced themselves from: Respect and Reverence for the laws of the Universe, rules not created or written by us. Last, it is not easy to accept that a human being is not the ruler of Nature, but only a particle given a certain time and place in the Universe and only loaned ideas and means towards self-fulfillment.

An awareness of many karmic outcomes has been awakened, starting with atonement for the extinct types of plants and animals and a feeling of happiness for the ones saved in time, such as buffalos and whales, before they became extinct. The understanding that there are other types of energy, which we haven't as yet learned how to detect and measure, gives us a sense of awareness of our presence on the chessboard of the Universe. The joy of knowing that we are not the only beings in the Universe already exists in scientific circles. There are theories about the transformation of one type of energy-matter into another. Everyone understands the irrevocable consequences of nuclear experiments and those who have gone through them know the effects of the tragedies on the next generations in Hiroshima and Chernobyl. Nature and the Universe do not forgive a violent intervention into their laws. The earth is an organ of some cosmic entity, but we are doing it harm by taking advantage of a temporary lack of self-control and non-union with Higher Forces over us. As we do damage to our planet in the form of wars and various fossil extractions, we forget about the eternity of cosmic and karmic laws.

The three true states present in the world keep it in balance: positive and negative, good and evil, health and disease. To choose which side you are on as you try to reach a specific goal completely depends on your life in the earlier ages. This choice affects both present and future lives as well as redemption for this decision.

One of my patients brought me a book of healing arts, saying that it describes my technique. I read this book with pencil in hand. During my enthusiastic reading, I initially imagined that the author was describing knowledge and experience unique to him. It took me a long time to research an enormous amount of related literature on healing, after which I came to the conclusion that nothing new has been discovered. Everything about the rules of healing has been known for a long time. The information accumulated by previous generations has been carried in waves to the new, more modern, way of understanding.

We must create a chain of knowledge. We are responsible for the transmission to our children and grandchildren of our experience and our ability to love all the things on earth. My parents in Belarus gave me the first lessons of respect towards Nature and utilization of its gifts. "Do not tear, break, but plant and help, and the compensation will come. If you hurt yourself, do not run after help, but put on a leaflet of a plantain; if you have a fever, drink a lime tea; if you get a small sunburn, put some sour cream on it; if it's too strong, dilute with some of your own urine or vegetable oil." Such lessons taught me and my siblings to rely more on Nature and ourselves rather than depend every minute on medicine. Ever since I have transmitted my experiences as well as those of my parents to the next generation, I cannot allow the chain of knowledge to stop.

Human experience and wisdom are accumulated through years and generations. The task of any healer is not to lose sight of this long-lived science – the folk wisdom – and to multiply its treasures. You may have heard: "If you spill the salt, there will be a quarrel." If salt is an actual absorber of negative energy, then this can be easily explained. Being spilled, it leads to expulsion of the emotions which were earlier absorbed by it. For example, my mother recommended keeping a sack of salt under a child's mattress. Salt is the absorber of negative information which can affect the infant. Salt as a crystal is specifically used in many cultures, starting with omens and superstitions and ending with the source of necessary minerals for our body.

We are able to explain some superstitions from both scientific and lay perspectives. Some of them no longer make sense, as the origins of their creation are lost in the whirl of history. On the other hand, we can say that some part of this knowledge is yet to be re-discovered. For example, does anyone remember how to cure tuberculosis? Since ancient times it has been known that kumiss, a drink prepared from fermented mare's milk, is a healing remedy for tuberculosis. The combination of inhaling fresh air with the drink of kumiss leads to astonishing results.

Also, what about healthy walks barefoot on the early morning's dew? Perhaps you will even take the chance to lie on the grass. Use your free time for enrichment of your energy potential through communion with Nature. The healer is granted a special fate: always to be on the alert, always to be conscious of everything going on around him or her. Communion with Nature must become a norm and be included in our daily routine instead of being a diversion only permitted on holidays. You do not have to be afraid of touching trees. It is so good to commune with Nature alone. Speak to a tree and you will receive answers to all your problems, if you only allow time for your soul to come in contact with it. Talk to it politely, with reverence, and the rewards will come.

Thanks to cooperation with Nature, the healer acquires skills, strength, and knowledge crucial to restore one's own resources and mobilize them for the well-being of those who need cures. The necessary life-giving energy descends either from the heights of space or ascends from the depths of the earth, the positive meeting the negative to form the neutral, the balanced. Knowledge of the laws of Nature becomes the expression of its love towards the seeker, and not everyone is allowed to possess it. If you have that knowledge, treat it with care; do not throw it around wastefully but transmit it to those who deserve it. To be chosen for the healing of the sick is to carry the cross of a blessed burden, not having a right to rest and to transgress from moral humane norms of existence. The smallest violation of laws, established from above by healers, leads to undesirable consequences, which are usually concealed by the healers themselves, who are aware of the cause. Certainly, I am no exception to this rule. Let me tell you what happened to me during my seemingly innocent attempt to help. While riding a bike in the park, I saw a father trying to help his daughter who had hurt her knee. Without thinking, I offered my services. Going towards them, I fell, together with the bike, on the sidewalk and hurt myself. I have never fallen from a bike before. My parents always said, "She rides like a boy. She does not know what caution is, and she never keeps her hands on the wheel."

For the first time I found myself in need of help. Suddenly, I understood – I was prevented from helping the child, my mission was to be available at this time for other people, the ones no one else could help.

I have written this book first for those going for an initial appointment with a healer, or those who have decided to improve their health without outside interference, and second for all those healers who seek support and strength in the uneasy, ungratifying, and at times dangerous struggle against dark forces in the process of therapy. I am thankful to all who have entered my life and shared anxious, yet invaluable experiences stemming from the treatment and contact with invisible forces of the **Quasiworld**.*

One day, I was in deep thought, contemplating the phenomena of invisible forces. Since everything must have a name, I felt this type of energy also needed a scientific name. For some unexplained reason, I fell into a deep trance. During that time "Quasiworld" came to mind as a name for this dimension. At first I could not understand, why this word? In Russia, 'quasi' is a physics term for elementary particles of molecular structure. It never occurred to me what this really meant. Minutes later, I awoke from my trance and immediately opened my dictionary to find that 'quasi' means 'invisible' or 'unreal.' I was astonished! Until this moment I never knew that 'quasi' meant 'invisible,' but accepted the name with all my heart. Those who already read my book in Russian are using this term to mean 'untouchable' or 'invisible.'

"Quasiworld" is my term for the genuine but invisible side of the Universe, which has existed forever and knows neither time nor space. It is the abode of the unconscious human mind and the source of paranormal phenomena.

The art of healing, in conjunction with the quasiworld, is the pinnacle of mastery, delivered from above and given to healers for the welfare of humanity. Many persons who have experienced the

---

*Quasi- – unreal; resembling but not being.

wondrous power of real healers and the healing influence of the
forces of the quasiworld describe their impressions with genuine
astonishment. They often cannot fully believe their experience.
They also cannot find fitting words to describe their internal or
external states during healing sessions.

Is there a scientific explanation for these quasifacts? It is
lacking because of our ignorance, and our fear of becoming
branded pseudo-scientists. Meanwhile, some scientific
"researchers" become our patients. During the sessions, they often
adopt a certain humility towards mysticism, and awe before their
initiation into the ancient secrets of the Universe.

I am confident that for readers who are not healers, this book
will open their hearts, for some – their souls, for others – their
minds to this new knowledge, particularly in the area of medicine
and treatment of disease. Everyone must develop a basic
knowledge and cultivate his or her abilities to pose honest
questions and not be afraid of the answers. We must also prepare
to seek second opinions or advice from alternative medical
practitioners. This is an option which has been a taboo among the
people of Western civilization for centuries, but it is increasingly
being chosen now.

When reading this book, don't be nervous to learn about things
which some people call "mystical or spiritual." Knowledge is
power! This power is inside each one of us! It's inside of you. You
have the capability and responsibility to make wise decisions.
Ignorance breeds fear. Give yourself a chance to get rid of your
fear of the unknown. Understanding the history of modern
medicine and of the healing arts of alternative medicine will give
you confidence. Ancient healing arts and modern medicine are not
necessarily enemies; they can compliment each other. Don't be
afraid to understand, learn about yourself and help yourself!

Knowledge is not destructive, but demands good judgment. It
then offers the opportunity to learn and helps one toward
understanding the wisdom of the ages. Readers who ask the right
question, who seek an honest answer and who do not fear the
truth, which may appear from the hidden past, will benefit from
the Healing Power of this book. Seek information as you take an
interesting and enlightening journey!

Chapter II

THE KARMA CYCLES

*As soon as questions of will or decision,
or reason, or choice of action arise,
human science is at a loss.*
                              —Noam Chomsky

Make The Change

*O*ur inner light increases every moment

No time to change the destiny of past
The world in which we live decreases
To change the evil into good
This is the way we try to live with others of our kind
The past has made the way for the future
The soul of life has not been judged
The living intellect will have the key
To open the way for us in hope
For the growth of our children
The strength of the past will help us in unfolding our destiny
The beings of our world will offer the change
This is the only thing we need
The change for future generations
That makes us what we must become
Not to ignore what has been and what will be.

N. Madorsky

We do not understand why children often are held responsible for the sins of their ancestors, and not the other way around, on this side of the world. However, we have the power to prevent such phenomena from occurring. Each of our deeds to humanity, nature, and the laws of being reflect in the mirror of eternity and have a place in the archives of the Macrocosm. Rewinding the tape of my memory and looking through the medical histories of my patients, I have noted that some people who have committed crimes against humanity do not feel any retribution during their lifetime. The burden falls on their children, grandchildren, and great-grandchildren, and so on, until the end of the line. The absence of children in a family due to economics, career, or health reasons is only a masked consequence. The true cause is known only to those who created the circumstances and those who observed the deed. Simultaneously the information was recorded in the lists of the Quasiworld.

The energy information released with the last breath of innocent crime victims settles down on the biofields of the culprits and executioners. What about the quasienergy of feelings proceeding from the hearts of victims' relatives? Quasienergy is always channeled by those alive to the entire lineage of the criminal. Therefore, one of my first recommendations to a cancer patient is to ask forgiveness from God for the crimes committed by previous generations. Through daily prayers, you will receive spiritual support from your ancestors with whom you are connected by eternal and invisible ties, and you will find yourself purged from the energy strata of the past.

Through prayers, you can remove the causes that initiated diseases and disasters tormenting your family line. By eliminating the cause on the karmic level, you can expel the disease, which is the effect on the physical field. All of us have a chance to restructure our way of thinking and our way of life, not only for our own health and welfare but also for our children, grandchildren, and so on.

I tried to remember when I first encountered the word "fate," as in "Everything is in fate's hands," "You can't escape fate," "You reap what you sow," "One is the master of one's fate." Some of these sayings are folk wisdom, repeated by friends and relatives, and others are from written sources. Despite some differences among them, these sayings and proverbs are bound by a common rule: some things are inevitable. Every action, deed, crime, or feat, negative or positive thinking, and even imagination are evaluated faithfully. Information is constantly being accumulated in the cells of the long-term memory of the cosmic computer. As a result of this accumulation and processing facts at the universal level, one of the main laws of philosophy is invoked: the transition from quantity into quality. Nature likes balance and tries to maintain it by any and all means. Although it is not always realized immediately, the action of nature's laws is inescapable.

The purpose of this chapter is to explore some principles of the influence of fate on our diseases. The accumulation of causes leads to a strong manifestation of consequences. Nature does not know the word "punishment" or "hatred;" it aspires only to equilibrium and harmony of all that exists in the Universe. From ancient times, people knew about these rigid natural laws and tried to abide by them at all costs. When circumstances forced departure from the letter of the law, those who broke it asked forgiveness from the spirits, or their gods, or from the omniscient God, knowing that the retribution for the deed would touch the doers themselves or their descendents in the future.

The Hindu philosophy calls this principle by a short, but energy-filled word, KARMA: the cause-effect law of the Universe. Many people believe there are no coincidences. A coincidence is an unrealized law. Whatever happens to us is the result of some effects proceeding from our deeds or from the actions of previous generations or our past lives.

The revelation of the meaning of Karma in the philosophical sense is not the purpose of this book. This topic has been studied for centuries in many parts of the world. Numerous books and monographs have been devoted to it. I will offer my observations on some typical cases for possible ways to influence the impact of fate on our health – if not completely, at least to lessen its manifestations for our descendants and us. It is quite possible that some will be capable of averting or alleviating the inevitable or perhaps stopping before the completion of a reckless deed. One may also have a chance meeting with someone who is allowed to influence fate directly through deep healing of karma.

I once heard a speech by the author of a book on self-healing through Buddhism. He was a handsome, youthful man, but had an unnatural hue to his skin. At the same time, I realized the reason: He had leukemia. When did he choose Buddhism? As a student, he had converted to Buddhism, when his troubled soul, in depression, did not receive support from his family and the surrounding social and religious environment.

I asked a question after his presentation. What did he think about reincarnation, as mentioned in his lecture, in light of redemption for one's trespasses, when, due to some psychological, political or material reasons, one has to renounce the faith of his ancestors to achieve well-being? Although in his lecture he had never mentioned the word "punishment" for the broken laws, the author confirmed my observations from practice and life. The Dalai Lama once mentioned to him the necessity to abide by the religious convictions of one's family.

How many years will pass before the burden of fate lands upon those who trespass the boundary? Becoming disillusioned from your family's beliefs for unclear reasons and choosing to adopt another philosophical or religious trend possibly occurred because of karma or even a physical cause. Family often does not accept the change and generates negative energy toward the individual. It is quite a different thing if one pursued purely selfish ends. Due to the laws of Being, the consequences of these changes are severe.

So why does karma play such an important part in our daily lives? The fact is, in comparison with cosmic time scales, our life has already been lived and more than one future rebirth is known. However, if we are given suitable warnings, we have the chance of correcting all that seems impossible to change. We are always granted an opportunity to struggle for change, which is encouraged. There is always one or another solution. Yet, do we know that only one real solution exists – the necessity of fighting for oneself?

Leukemia is one of the diseases which involves suffering for the atonement of misdeeds that occurred in one's past life, as well as in the present life. Leukemia does not know any age limits. It is quite probable that the betrayal of one's principles and views does not always agree with the collective opinion of a social group. The energetic impact of this clash leads to tragic consequences. The mental message is incorporated into the energy-information field of the receiver, thus distorting his inner energy potential.

What had a cute little girl who went to kindergarten with my children done wrong? At five, she was diagnosed with leukemia. At seven, she died. In her family, there was not a history of cancer, but her grandfather knew very well about murder. He had killed more than once in his zealous execution of military orders. He took pleasure in his power over life and death, killing civilians along with the enemy. It was his emotional attachment to the crime that created the negative energy field around his family.

When we are young, we do not realize the irrevocability of the laws of Being, and when understanding arrives, it is often too late. In many cases, the accumulation of infractions does not amount to critical mass during one lifetime – it requires several generations, the ones linked genetically, as well as the ones connected with the actions of a soul in previous incarnations.

What can one do if neither the mother nor her 12-year-old daughter Lynn knows about the imminent leukemia, while only her aunt and I were intuitively aware of it? Lynn merely continues the chain of oncological conditions on her father's side of the family. For now, one can only wait for the manifestation of the disease in this cheerful, seemingly healthy, athletic girl.

In another family with whom I am well acquainted, the recollections about past generations are maintained with honor and respect. But why have they suddenly been stricken by a chain of accidents and diseases, ending with cancer in the preceding generation and continuing now among the cousins? How had all this negative energy accumulated here? Perhaps someone planted a curse upon this family? Perhaps the karma cycles brought a stranger into their line, who, in the name of the word "inheritance," made a terrifying oath, never realizing the tragic consequence?

Everything is connected in this world. A focused mental message of negative, concentrated energy leads to disintegration of the defensive energy field created for centuries. The impact is passed on to the next generation. A rupture of family ties leads to a weakening of defense mechanisms in the members of a social group. This knowledge, accumulated through centuries, is no longer passed on orally in many parts of the world. The best hope of gaining this knowledge is through available materials. A humble reverence to the wisdom of the elders, which earlier helped in creating and maintaining the energy shield, is diminishing, initiating the degradation of the younger generations in both moral and physical aspects.

A young woman named Irene asked her mother for help in caring for her newborn. In spite of her own physical exhaustion, her mother could not refuse. Her unexpressed desire to say, "No," was so great that deliverance unexpectedly came to her in the form of a very acute illness. Mentally breaking karma's law, her mother began to endure its consequence through a disease with indescribable spells of pain and suffering, coming from nowhere and surprising the doctors. While her mother was hospitalized, Irene was forced to care for her newborn and her handicapped father, and visited her mother daily. If we look in great detail at the causes of a rare disease, we see that it can sometimes be explained as an effect of negative thinking by parents toward their children. The lesson from this is simple: No matter what happens, parents should love their children and children should love their parents.

Nature reacts to this situation in its own way, bestowing suffering as a reply to unwillingness. As we see, the beginning of the disease is the consequence of disruption and avoidance of the Laws of Nature. When Irene returned home with her child, a miracle occurred. Her mother's health drastically improved. One can see how elimination of the cause that started the disease can lead to change in the effect. If Irene had continued to stay in her parents' house, her mother would have drifted from one diseased state to the next. Irene's merit rests in her awareness of the cause and the removal of unpleasant consequences.

In this example, the daughter had correctly understood the situation. In most cases, however, the causes are very difficult to identify. They are present within us – our deeds, our thinking, our way of life, and in our relationships with the surrounding reality. We have difficulty admitting that we are the creators and carriers of not only our own diseases but also the diseases of those to whom we are closely bound. It demands psychological exertion and mobilization of all our mental strength.

The use of the word "karma" is inevitably accompanied by examples from previous incarnations. The majority of current relationships have already been made in previous lives, and the majority of effects of present situations are hidden in past causes. Sometimes we do not understand why an otherwise nice person is unpleasant to us; we feel as though some old incident has come between us and still does not give us peace. However, in other cases, first contact with another person feels almost like a celebration. We are ready to communicate with him always, intuitively knowing that he can be trusted and wouldn't abandon us in trouble. The karmic bonds are not easy to break if they are created through strong emotions. A huge effort is needed to build unseverable bonds between human beings, bonds so strong that they can be passed from one incarnation to another, from a previous generation to the next one.

An accidental meeting with a young man named Harry at a business seminar developed into a one-hour conversation. A year later, I received an anxious telephone call requesting an appointment. It had taken a year for Harry to realize he needed help. During our first meeting, I perceived a sign of his karmic disease. But who wants to hear about something that is not yet a danger? His determination to see me proved to be quite opportune. If he had waited only a couple of months, the result would have been tragic. It took only a few sessions to restore the normal activity of his immune and endocrine systems. Now his progress depends on him, on his wish to pursue and fulfill his objectives in this life.

An unusual detail came to light in studying our karmic bonds. He had saved my life in a near-death situation during one of his previous incarnations. The laws maintain harmony and balance: it was my turn to save his life.

For a while, Harry had searched for someone who could give him assistance. When we met, neither of us had ever been at such a seminar before. Due to the circumstances, I found myself for the first and last time at that particular place where I met him. Not everyone is allowed to receive timely help. It is necessary to earn it in previous generations.

Leo had been my long-time friend and has helped me many times, I was not able to help him when he needed it. One time when I met him for lunch, his usual smoker's cough sounded different. I became alarmed. Immediately, I decided to mentally scan him. I detected lung cancer. I consulted the universal information field, the Higher Power, for permission to treat Leo. But, the reply was negative: I was forbidden to treat him. Because I knew I was not allowed to treat him, I did not tell him of his condition. To my regret, I could not save him from his fate, perhaps because he did not desire to fight or perhaps his grandparents betrayed their religion for a comfortable life. Why did I never experience a feeling of compassion and a desire to aid him, even though we saw each other regularly? We are helpless when we realize our limits in methods, means, and access in giving assistance to those who need it. Actually, nature has put constraints on both my choice of friends, as well as patients.

One infertile couple looked for help in all the medical institutions that they could find, but help arrived only after they adopted two infants. In exactly nine months after this event, they gave birth to their own son. Another couple decided not to have children, preferring careers over having a family. Their karmic lesson took almost thirty years for the oncological disorders to reach them. Time can never be reversed, but we are always capable of fixing our errors, of balancing our accounts. In order to change our future, we must be willing to analyze our imperfections at any particular moment and begin the healing process for the body or soul.

Leah had developed negative emotions towards her family since her childhood. Many years passed before she perceived a sign of inevitable karmic disease. In the beginning, it manifested a pre-cancerous state with prominent changes in the mucous membrane of her rectum. Medical help was given in time, but her spiritual worldview was never re-evaluated.

As a middle-aged woman, Leah had forgotten about the warning, and again a signal of a pre-cancerous state appeared, but this time in the pancreas. At that time, Leah, who was more interested in material comforts, ignored the warnings about her health and need for spiritual growth. I do not think the higher forces will spend their time reminding her to re-evaluate her spiritual beliefs. Only we are responsible for the most precious thing that exists in nature – our health.

I am convinced this was not the first karmic lesson that Leah had received. From life to life, this lesson will continue until she derives meaning from it. She didn't learn from the deaths of her grandfather and uncles, from both maternal and paternal lines, together with several cousins from cancer. All attempts to persuade Leah to slow down and care not only for herself, but also for her only child, who also needed maternal attention, did not succeed.

Her spouse also had cancer, but in a more advanced stage. This struck me as odd, for her husband was from a family known for longevity and he had never been sick. His wife's cells responded to the vibration from her husband's unhealthy body, and now she had cancer too. Finding the same disease in a couple suggests to me the matrimony of the cancer cells on the micromolecular or energetic level.

There is one more interesting observation connected with this couple. Years ago, they purchased a home where the previous owners had died from cancer. The whole house was affected by stifling negative energy, from which there was only one escape – leaving. It is quite possible that the house was situated in a biopathogenic zone, which stimulated otherwise healthy cells to rebel against the regulating life-support systems.

Although she was knowledgeable in alternative medicine and had referred friends to practitioners, Leah proved unprepared to deal with her own disaster. Cancer is a special condition which, once active, does not easily retreat. Through the disintegration of the nervous system, it slowly takes over more territory for its existence.

Such cases require the intervention of an individual who is competent and capable of directing bioenergy currents to the specific areas fighting the cancer cells. Whether I will have a chance to help Leah, I don't know, but I am sure the situation she is facing raises an inevitable question: "Is it worthwhile, and does God want it...?" Since when have material goals started prevailing over the spiritual? Pause for an instant, look around you, and contemplate the meaning of our existence on earth. Why and for whom is it necessary to worship God and obey His command?

The correlation on the karmic level between spouses is not always recognized. Only awareness of the serious influence of previous incarnations on the present and the future impacts the flow of events. Not much is needed for that – only to embrace the eternal laws of the Universe. This faith allows us to take a step toward the restoration of the natural exchange of energy currents between spouses.

I have often observed how people prepare themselves to receive a disease which they have previously confronted in their family surroundings, without contemplating the possibility of avoiding it. Such self-hypnosis resembles the behavior of the mesmerized rabbit in front of a boa constrictor. When we don't pay attention to our body, we find it easy to absorb negative information from those who are sick. It does not matter how this connection is manifested. Several possibilities exist: actual physical contact, an energy effect from a distance based on the resonance of the "biocontour" frequencies of the members of one's family, or energy levels raised by handling objects belonging to the sick person. From birth, we have the ability to change our destiny, if we would only listen to our internal voice in time and consider the information in our possession! Alas, not everyone is capable of turning the wheel of fortune backwards. In most cases, our outlook and experience lead us to conform to social requirements. Who can judge better than ourselves what we need in a particular situation for such a unique organism as our body? We are in charge of corrections! If we cannot make decisions in such cases, then who can make them? The knowledge of what is best for us is implanted instinctually by Mother Nature.

It is interesting to look at the cases concerning sick doctors. There is nothing consistent about them. Some are aggressively disposed against methods not studied in medical schools; yet others, admitting philosophically to the limits of current therapeutic practices, make efforts in search of alternative forms of treatment. Nature always gives us a chance, and our will consists of making a choice, which hopefully will be the right one.

I have observed the plight of a certain physician, Dorian, for three or four years. My first meeting with her had alerted me, and the following ones confirmed my suspicions. Her talkativeness – often without making any sense – the clear changes of the energy field around her body, and her emaciated features were only the tip of the iceberg. A year later, I warned Dorian about the danger I sensed and the urgency of taking measures against it. I had performed local testing and discovered the familiar energy of oncologic aberrations in the area of the pancreas. Then I asked about her family history. Her mother had died from cancer when Dorian was a child. As in many cases, because of disrespect for her health and constant lack of time, Dorian could not find a minute to be alone with herself.

More than a year and a half passed before we met again, and it was hard to recognize her. This time I was told that she had diabetes, which indicates a dysfunction in the pancreas. Again, I pointedly reminded her about the seriousness of her situation. Dorian asked me to reveal my concerns. Worried about her children, I decided to tell her the truth as I saw it. A sudden and powerful reaction followed. Many of her relatives had gone through the same ordeal, and she did not differ from them in any respect. Generally there is no cure for pancreatic cancer. Furthermore, she did not believe in a chance of recovery. I tried to remind Dorian once more that everything was in her hands and that one has to start with prayer, which can produce a spiritual revolution. After that, it will become apparent what measures are required to counteract her condition.

The conversation ended when it became apparent to me that Dorian had made her choice at the time of her mother's death. Such a fate is often more familiar and easier to handle than those where the roads are obscured. I try honestly to warn people of the impending danger and offer ways to avoid it, but if there is no desire on the patient's part to pay attention, nothing can be done.

As the saying goes: "Any disease, in principle, can be cured, but not every patient can." Karma performs its job in maintaining order in the laws of being. In one case, destiny reminds us about the inescapability of repeating an unlearned lesson, but at other times, the cosmos gives rewards and sends deliverance from a menacing disease in the form of indispensable knowledge or an unexpected teacher. The challenge rests with the perception, acknowledgment, and interpretation of the signs of fate. I very rarely try to give notice of unfolding danger to people I meet casually. As I have noted, I feel strongly only when our paths have intersected in previous incarnations.

From the first moment I talked with Kelly, I was amazed at the pleasant energy field that surrounded her. The affinity was so great that, for an instant, the perception of a deep sadness emanating from her soul was mollified. The links to previous incarnations are much stronger than we acknowledge. Experiences in previous lives bring people by mysterious paths to meetings with healers and recovery from sickness. As I learned later, in one of my earlier incarnations I had had close blood ties with Kelly. The hidden memory of the past had led her to me again.

The diagnosis confirmed our worst suspicions: Cancer. I cannot forget this case because it is one of the few in my practice where the malignant transformations emerged simultaneously in three seemingly unconnected organs. It required two sessions per day in order to produce an effect.

I'd like to emphasize that only Kelly's faith in the accuracy of the diagnosis, which she confirmed, and her belief in the first mental imagery session of treating her internal organs with sunlight, as I recommended, allowed her to mobilize her internal resources to defend her body against hostile, rampant cells. Kelly was a skeptic by nature, but she wisely decided to fight with all available means. She took seriously all the recommendations dealing with restructuring her way of thinking, behavior, religious preference, and mental and physical exercises, along with diet, without exception. Perhaps the repeated signs of unexpected weakness, bloody discharges and other aberrations forced Kelly to rely on ancient knowledge as well as official medicine.

The next example demonstrates the interdependence of reincarnations and the subsequent actions directed at correcting broken universal laws renounced by previous generations. A young woman, named Daisy, came to me because of her persistent headaches. The doctors could not find anything. The disorder was in an early stage and could not be diagnosed. Her intuitive husband had given a correct diagnosis: inflammation of the body. In this case, I witnessed a change in karma made by a living member of an older generation that had initiated the effect upon the younger one.

The first indication of danger had been received several years before in the form of unsuccessful pregnancies. Further attempts to have children were blocked by an accelerating inflammation throughout her body. I was able to link the disease to spiritual reconstruction of this brilliant woman. After I investigated the causes of the disease, it became clear that neither past lives nor previous generations had anything to do with it. Her own mother and the negative energy she generated were the culprits. Before Daisy was born, her mother had an abortion which was not a part of the cosmic plan. After many years, the karmic retribution for this insensitive deed had come by God's will. Fortunately for Daisy, she had a chance to change everything. She needed only faith in her own abilities and in the reality of the existence of the higher laws.

Here another story about one couple whom I knew quite well and was aware of some aspects of their family history. After he arrived in the United States from Germany after World War II, Sam married a young woman whose family hailed from the Ukraine. He was originally from Russia and had worked as a guard in the German concentration camps. This man, with a robust complexion, had never been sick, but met his end in lung cancer. His two daughters were doomed to childlessness. Their mother tried to make amends for her husband's guilt for the sake of her daughters. She volunteered daily caring for old people who were victims of the war. Who is the judge of this situation? Maybe only his children...

Then, how can one deal with Ted and Matt, whose fathers served in the Nazi army and had committed more than one inhuman act? Their beautiful children are repaying this debt with cancer, in the trial of generations. If the young ones and their older European ancestors had known about the link between events, then the situation might have been somewhat different. Almost all the families of the pre-war era belonged to religious communities, and they should have known about the effect of crimes against humanity upon the lives of following generations. These views and convictions, coming from bitter experience, can be found in religious teachings through millennia. One of the ten commandments of the Old Testament says: "Thou shall not kill".

The following story tells about a long way to restore the activity of the immune and endocrine systems during the treatment of one young, vigorous girl named Laura. Due to the lack of precise information, her doctors were damaging her systems with strong medications. The damage changed her life. Laura's parents had to be involved in the process of healing. Without their spiritual rebirth, there could be no improvement. Powerful karmic fluctuations from several generations before Laura's birth came into play. She could only be helped by the combined efforts of her relatives and the support of invisible spiritual allies. They are the ones who come to us with words in the most difficult times, possessing a real power of assistance. These are the phrases which we seem to utter in delirious states.

I asked several times for assistance from the Higher Power. The prayer Laura had to recite came to me after several requests. It was given to me for the salvation of this striking red-haired girl. How much sacrifice had Laura made working as a volunteer in a hospital? The cosmic gratitude for the invaluable work came when it seemed that she could not expect any help. Such quite simple words, which are capable of helping in the difficult moments, are shown below, for future needs:

Prayer for Help*

God, I ask You to protect me from devilish schemes.
God, I am ready to join You in fighting
my ailment and black force.
I release my pain for reasons that I do not grasp yet.
God, to care for myself is most important for me.
Lord, help me, in your ways. You can do that!
Lord, all that I need now is to feel You in my soul.
Lord, find the paths that are destined for me – it is my trial.
Lord, open for me the doors to the future.
Lord, attend to me! Attend! Attend!
Amen! Amen! Amen!

I recall another patient, Nick, with family karmic lessons. A number of interesting details came to light during our talks while he was undergoing biotherapy. This is a pure and typical karmic example of the interdependence of previous incarnations and generations, those still living and those already gone, and their influence on the future generations.

Nick's father renounced the faith that his ancestors had carried with pride through the centuries in order to embrace another, due entirely to economic motives. Nick's father, grandmother, and aunt were confronted with a form of cancer afterwards. Nick himself was unconsciously tempted to commit a crime without any meaning, but each time some force held him back.

---

* Prayer of R. Madorsky

Revisiting his previous lives only confirmed the worst fears. In the 17th century, he was a disreputable murderer who feared neither God nor devil. Murders were committed to satisfy insatiable, base passions. In his current long life, despite all indications to the contrary, Nick showed himself as a true champion of health and honorably filled his place in society. Regrettably, this was not the case with his children. His daughter experienced poor health. She gave birth to a child who died in Nick's arms a week later. At almost the same time as this tragic event happened, the daughter underwent cardiac surgery during which a mistake occurred. The aorta was confused with the vena cava. This was discovered instantly after the heartbeat was reactivated, so the surgery was performed again. How she survived all that, only God knows. Nick's son had his own sad bout with drug abuse, which is still being written with an unknown denouement. The perpetuation of Nick's lineage is currently facing a big question. Karma again – one must be astonished by it.

The following case is of special significance. I became acquainted with Julia at a friend's gathering. Julia was also writing a book about her own healing experiences. Our views differed. Our conclusions corresponded to our different perspectives of our patients' problems. Towards the end of our encounter, Julia asked me to examine her, explaining she was interested in different methods of diagnosis. She confirmed my diagnosis, as she knew what to expect and was prepared. To my surprise, Julia insisted on immediate treatment. The process was initiated. The cause lay in her husband, who was also affected with the corrosive effect of cancer. While checking his karma, I could not establish any reasons for the manifestation of negative forces. It was the first such incident in my long practice! He was only being punished for not lending needed support to his wife in her effort to improve the moral state of her soul. As soon as he tried to help her, everything returned to normal for him. This case was unusual because of the insight into karmic relationships between spouses.

Each time I work with a new patient, I devote time in the initial session to unraveling the reasons that led to the onset of disease and examining the bonds arising from previous generations and previous reincarnations. Throughout the treatment, a slow spiritual transformation occurs, together with the realization for the need of change in the soul. I cannot even talk about healing if the patient will not embrace a feeling of tender love and respect towards himself as an individual. This is the key to the healing process.

To achieve self-respect, I recommend looking in the mirror and talking with your reflection as you would with a close friend. Speak about your worries and how you respect and love yourself despite physical or other deficiencies. Tell yourself that your love grows proportionately to the number of wrinkles on the face, folds on the stomach, and with each ailment. You can promise to be loyal to yourself and give complete support in the process of recovery. The "I" that knows all that has happened in previous incarnations and generations will receive invaluable information through such conversations and will retain it forever. Make this self-contact every morning or evening as often as possible, and you start to revive. The destiny of each of us resembles a delicate cobweb, woven from billions of thoughts, deeds and epiphanies that happened to us, our relatives, our friends and everyone whose roads we intersect during our life on this planet. The fate of our ancestors leaves a red trail on our life, whether we realize it or not, and the fates of our children are shaped by our deeds. Both positive and negative information is unconsciously transmitted to us as we resume the race with karma. It is worthy to note that as soon as we recognize the phenomenon of general interdependence, the sparks of recovery immediately manifest themselves.

Each of us is in charge not only of our own actions, creation of our own karma, destiny or fate, but for how they affect every human being in the present as well as the future. The results of deeds, planted in the past, will develop in the future generations. When we face the truth, we can change our fate.

Chapter III

ANOTHER WAY TO KNOWLEDGE

*In the mechanics of nature, everything in the
Universe is connected with everything else.*
                                    —Maxine Asher

*Health is not a condition of matter, but of
Mind; nor can the material senses bear
reliable testimony on the subject of health.*
                                    —Mary Baker Eddy

The Chance

The smoke is in the sky like clouds

It is the time to live the life
The blackest darkest black is at its end
We must decide our fate of life
We are the makers of the death.
The days are in, we are in charge
The power struggle will continue
There is no choice in what we do
We must decide on how we'll do it.
Since the beginning of time
We had a chance to be in power
The chance had passed us in a flash
The time will come again for us to take
The future seed of past itself.
We have to plant the life inside
There is a place for us to go
To find that place we must survive
Survive the struggle of the ages.

N. Madorsky

Cancer patients present the most difficult cases in the healing process. I dispute some established opinions and hypotheses involving our attitudes toward our loved ones and ourselves. In any given case, not only is the healer faced with the task of inhibiting the process of cancer cell division and augmenting the activity of the immune system, but must also aid the patient in re-evaluating his or her moral values, world understanding and reality perception. In the recovery process, all of the inner substance is changing along with attitudes toward being and consciousness as unalterable factors in the Universe.

My experience, an accumulation of many years of practice with cancer patients, allows me to contribute to the clarification of the causes of the appearance, as well as the reasons for the disappearance, of this terrifying disease. The information has grown out of observations and conversations with loved ones, relatives, friends, colleagues, and patients. Some I knew before they were diagnosed by orthodox methods; others, afterwards. Some came to me tormented by inner fears. I am not competent to answer all questions about the causes of cancer in various groups of people, but I feel it is my duty as a healer to share my personal observations.

No other disease demands such sheer exertion of psychological and moral strength as cancer. The structuring of connections between the past and current generations is a profound task. Everything is interlocked in Nature and the Universe that one is not only awestruck, but simply doesn't know how to make humanity aware of the overall situation. Only philosophy can handle this task; it combines all accessible knowledge under one heading. It can easily explain effects with its concepts and contents and logically derive their meaningful correlations.

There are many speculations regarding the etiology of cancer, and even more on the methods of treatment. As yet, there is no absolute way of preventing this often terminal illness. For centuries, humanity has tried to solve this problem. Why are some families, or even whole clans, prone to oncological disorders up to the extinction of the line, but others are bypassed by cancer in all generations? Why, at some moment, do the seemingly healthy cells go out of control and transform into cancerous ones?

Most applied sciences derived from philosophy are based on the interpretation of natural processes, the study of phenomena with the help of instrumentation, and often preoccupied with specific ideas and concepts. The mysteries of Nature are endless, and much remains unknown of historical development at this time. Perhaps we are not ordained to know some things in the name of preservation of the human race. In fact, the necessary technical devices for measurement of many familiar and still scientifically unexplained phenomena have not been invented, *psi* phenomena, for example. Otherwise, it would be possible to show those who don't believe in the supernatural foundations that the human being is the microcosm in the macrocosm.

Modern investigations have verified that the frequencies of energy field oscillations generated by each organ differ from each other, as do the frequency fluctuations resulting from disease. Cancer cells are programmed to vibrate with a frequency exactly like that of the human embryo. Due to this, life-support systems in the body start supplying resources to the cancer cells, leading to their proliferation. The immune systems defending us from unforeseen changes fall into the trap. The immune and endocrine systems are drained. That is why it is very important to stimulate these two systems and reformulate the information fields of all organs and tissues affected by the disease.

The American biochemist, Glenn Rein, in conducting research at Queen Charlotte's Hospital in London, used Kirlian techniques in studying tissue samples from women with and without breast cancer. Rein discovered that the brightness of luminescence emitted by the abnormal breast tissue was more intense than the luminescence of the healthy samples. Rein went further and discovered that the hands of cancer patients release more energy than those of patients in good health. Some scientists hypothesize that the release of a significant quantity of energy by cancer patients attests to the transition of the body into the state of degeneration and, therefore, the loss of the ability to maintain vigor.

Also, scientist David Cohen from the Massachusetts Institute of Technology affirms the dependence of the human electromagnetic field, or aura, on the internal state of the subject. The link between health, mood, mental disposition, and the chromatic corona enfolding the person has been established. For example, a person with cancer generates an expanded, dispersed corona, while a healthy person produces a lucid, concentrated one.

The world's dream is to find the panacea for cancer in this century. However, I am ready to venture that mankind's deliverance from cancer is not too far away. The road to this deliverance is before our eyes. I know that it is hard to believe and difficult to understand with our current mindset.

During the impact of the energy-spiritual treatments, the vibration frequency of the damaged organs is restored to an acceptable magnitude, and they have a chance to attain a sufficient energy potential for the forthcoming fight with the cancer. After that build up, the body can distinguish the presence of the masked abnormality and begin to struggle with the disease, withdrawing energy from dangerous cancerous tissues. Life force is directed only into healthy tissues and the immune system, thus disarming the opponent. When the cancer cells do not have a chance to use resources at the expense of neighboring tissues, they slowly retreat. In this decisive moment of the battle, strong cooperation between the patient and the healer is very important. In cases where the cancer process is on the visual diagnostic level, the same can be applied by the physician.

During the hands-on energetic diagnosis of the patient, my warning signals are an unpleasant pinching at the end of the fingers or palms, the feeling of touching dry ice, or the feeling of a vacuum in one or another organ. These unusual sensations signal the beginnings of malignant formations. These perceptions are perhaps caused by the presence of special radioactive emissions discharged by cancer cells during their multiplication. In such cases, I always re-check the subtle energy information by connecting myself psychically to the cosmic information field, my Higher Power. If the information is confirmed, I recommend, without exception, that this person consult a medical specialist. However, in initial stages, it is often very difficult or even impossible to validate my information even by modern diagnostic methods. The perceived signals not only warn me, but also force me to become aware of the presence of something undesirable masked behind the facade of healthy organs. I have to trust my own professional intuition.

In most cases, the patients do not consciously feel the approach of the illness, or they suppress their suspicions deeply in the passages of their unsettled souls. Usually people come to me with diseases and symptoms completely unrelated to cancer, but these symptoms are the first defense signals of the organism. There are several hypotheses of the origin of oncologic disorders:

- Genetic mutations on the cellular level.
- Manifestation of Nature's law – Karma.
- Afflictions of the soul, not of the body, but arising in the context of apparent or hidden stress or guilt.
- Faulty exchange of energy information on the cellular level between component systems of the organism in a person or among family   members and others.
- Penetration of destructive information from various sources into healthy organisms at an energy informational level.
- Stimulation of healthy cells into rebellion via radioactive or other types of energy emissions.

There are many causes, more than those mentioned above, but the consequences are dangerous. The most important factor to the healer is to establish the primary source of disorder in the patient. Some causes, such as the repetition of life situations in past and present generations and the impact of the patients' past lives on the current one, are discussed in other chapters. The cancer cells are responsive to the same psychological effects as healthy ones. They react to commands sent by the mind, and one can see amazing results by acting upon them in a certain energy-spiritual way.

Often, in a seemingly helpless situation, a strong spiritual shock will make us think about the length of existence in this world and about the limitations of our mission. One of my patients, in response to an opinion about the unimportance of life expectancies, reflected: "All of us will die sooner or later. But, the later, the better."

A major key to the diagnosis of subtle malignant formations in the absence of perceivable irritants is the appearance of painful sensations in the suspected area during and after energy infusion by the healer. As mentioned before, the self-protective biochemical processes in malignant tissues deprive these areas of needed energy. The sudden flow of the excess energy to the ailing body, by the healer's efforts, drastically activates the defensive systems, unmasking the hidden unhealthy processes and provoking sudden painful sensations.

With each new patient, I immerse myself in an entirely new world of emotions and unique approaches to the healing. People vary, as do their emotional reactions to bad news, especially if the information is received from a professional without a medical degree. However, to be a doctor by degree does not mean to be one from birth.

The medical schools mainly teach an anatomical/physiological approach to treating human beings, assuming that all people possess the same anatomical and psychological system, and fail to remember that each patient is different. They deny the traditional wisdom of healers, accumulated through millennia and preserved in human society despite harsh persecution and discrimination from science and religious authority that have attempted control over what is truly priceless – the health and life of a human being. However, due to the increased use of treatment with chemical substances in modern medicine, we now see a re-evaluation of attitudes toward the use of those enduring, curative powers from folk medicine.

I will begin with one of the most interesting cases of healing that I have witnessed, confirmed by materials from medical investigations and the patient's participation in an experimental group to test a new method of medical treatment.

The history of Danielle's cancer and the process of her recovery is a classic example of the struggle for life where one can trace a path back to spiritual reincarnation. During the onset of cancer, she had all the attributes common in my experience to patients of this type. Danielle's mother died from lung cancer during the 80th year of her life, and several cousins died from ovarian cancer. Another cousin has also recently been diagnosed with the same condition.

During the previous three years, Danielle had been under strong psychological stress linked to family circumstances. She was also affected by a deep spiritual trauma from childhood. She kept it inside herself all her life, only occasionally blurting it out. She did not know what love is, how it can be manifested in close relationships, or how to react open-heartedly to demonstrations of love. Her main trouble was a complete disbelief in higher forces. She was brought up in an atheistic family, possibly without any deep moral values.

She was examined by a doctor for abdominal pain and constrained breathing. Danielle was diagnosed with ovarian cancer of the third stage, with metastases to the liver and diaphragm. She was given a zero chance for survival. After a hysterectomy, she was left with scattered metastases less than one centimeter in size surrounding the surgery area, and also with the metastases in her liver and diaphragm.

Danielle personally investigated the types of chemotherapy that might yield the best results and chose one recommended by the National Institute of Health and by her gynecological-oncological group. She had a total of eight sessions of chemotherapy. My offer to assist her was initially received skeptically. Nonetheless, our good relationship and her trust allowed me to begin my work with her. I had to use patience and persistence to assure her of the necessity of biotherapy sessions. She had nothing to lose.

By the time I started my work with her, she had already undergone one chemotherapy session. It took months to change her outlook on the essence of being. No matter how much you are involved with religious organizations or how much time you spend on the accomplishment of various projects, nothing will be changed if you do not restructure your inner spiritual meaning, directed toward real love and understanding of human nature and higher forces whose will we obey.

It is very difficult to convey what my inner state was while working with her. Only one thing I am sure of: one must never try to persuade anyone to use folk methods of treatment. Danielle was the most complicated person to heal in my experience. Despite Danielle's negative personality, even her friends encouraged me to continue the healing sessions with her. Many times I promised myself that it was my last session with her. Every time I returned, knowing that it was imperative to complete what was begun and that punishment from my Higher Power for unfinished business awaited me if I did not continue. This point I grasped only later. But at the beginning, I had to go through a trial from above for breaking some unknown universal laws. This happened in one of the earliest sessions with Danielle.

Once, upon finishing a session, I raised my hands with extended palms above her head. For the first time, at the height of 30-50 cm or 12-20 inches, I suddenly felt an inexpressible pain filling my hands and arms up to the shoulders. The sensation of twisting, inhuman pain was quite something, even for one who had born three children. I could not believe such unreal and unnatural sensations.

I repeated the position of the hands several times, until I became convinced that it wasn't a hallucination but, indeed, reality. Thus, I was given a warning in the very beginning that not everyone is in need of a helpful hand and that the helper can be stopped before it's too late. Until that incident, I never paused to ask the question about whether everyone is permitted to be cured or allowed to heal, or if they still have to learn some lesson in life through the anguish of disease. On that day, I felt a draining away of my strength and inexplicable weakness. I started to perform intensive breathing exercises and spent a long time outside in communion with nature to recover from an unpredictable lesson from above. In spite of this, I continued to work with her.

One night, after working with Danielle I woke up at 2:30 a.m. with internal disturbances. I "saw" a vision, if one can say that, in the upper corner of my bedroom. A group of people were sitting at a table discussing actions of mine that opposed certain cosmic laws. The conversation was serious and I intuitively grasped that my destiny was being decided upon. My right to live was questioned because of my work with a person whose fate had been established from above. No one could come to save me.

This was so captivating that I almost missed a moment when an entity, not participating in the discussion, and without consulting the others, threw a thin, weightless veil upon my body. In the same instant, I perceived a special feeling of spiritual protection.

I had been given a strong lesson from above: don't enter into conflict with laws of nature. From then on, before preparing to heal a new patient, I always ask for permission from the Creator to work with the patient and abide by that rule.

After one chemotherapy session at the hospital, Danielle had been in bed at home for several days when I came over to inquire about her health and perform a healing session. Danielle gave the impression of a person living the last minutes of her life. She couldn't raise herself to drink water, nor to take food.

Near the end of the healing session, Danielle suddenly sat up, drank some water, and then jumped up to take a shower, something she hadn't done during the past week. All of this happened as if in a dream, as if she hadn't been dying a minute before.

When I cautioned her that it was crucial to treat the session warily, she only grinned. The next day, she went to a restaurant to celebrate a friend's birthday.

Sessions with Danielle were always difficult. During my work with Danielle after one of her first chemotherapy sessions, the flame of a candle rose to the height of 15-20 cm. I pointed this phenomenon out to her, telling her that her negative energy, together with the energy of the toxic chemicals, was being consumed by the flame.

A burning candle is a constant presence in my working space. It is my reliable friend, assistant, and indicator. In all religious and ethnic rituals, fire performs a basic task in the creation of a zone filled by currents of the purest energy.

After three or four months, the cancer signals transmitted by my patient disappeared. The results of a scheduled medical test showed no new cancer formations as well as complete disappearance of the unremoved metastases. Because Danielle chose experimental cancer treatment from a well-known medical facility, she was obligated to have a second operation. The follow-up surgery confirmed total absence of metastasis. Biopsies also confirmed the absence of cancer cells in Danielle's body.

Years have passed since she became free from her consuming illness. Below are some impressions from Danielle's journal about the impact of biotherapy written about a month before her second operation. "Rachel Madorsky, a healer and teacher of BioEnergy Therapy, has been treating me for over six months. She began treating me after I had surgery for ovarian cancer and I was undergoing chemotherapy treatments. These treatments seem to help my immune system and allow me to be symptom-free between the chemo-procedures. My post-treatment CT scan shows no significant tumors, other than some fatigue and hair loss after the 2nd and 3rd taxol treatments, but I did not have significant side effects or symptoms after each of my eight chemotherapy treatments. My blood counts which were low immediately after treatment, always moved within a more acceptable range within two or three weeks. I suffered no infections during this period and I was able to tolerate all the treatments. Although I was in very good physical health prior to developing cancer, I was under a great deal of stress for a period of three years. Although there is no proof that bioenergy therapy alone accounted for my good results, I can recommend Ms. Madorsky and the therapy as a useful complementary treatment to traditional medicine. Ms. Madorsky has a natural skill as a healer and I believe that her method can produce positive physical and mental results."

In extreme situations, the healer has the closest ties with the patient, and he, the healer, perceives the disaster with his heart, unhumbled, undaunted by the struggle. After the absence of cancer cells was established, I supplied her with a list of other healers, wishing her luck.

Throughout my entire experience with the recuperation process from serious conditions like Danielle's, it became clear to me that it is important to integrate the efforts of the patient and the people close to her with those of the healer who would supply the missing cosmic energy to support the immune and endocrine systems during the initial stages of fighting the disease.

In most cases, full cooperation between the sick person and the healer is rarely achieved. The sick person has learned to rely on doctors or other professionals for his healing, when in reality he bears the primary responsibility for maintaining his health. The objectives of both the doctor and the healer are the same; only the roads and means leading to them are different. The will of the patient to recover plays a crucial role in the transformation and healing.

I met Jim at one of the conferences where I was invited to give a demonstration of my own techniques. During his diagnosis, I spotted the subtle signal of early stage cancer in his right kidney. I advised him to see his doctor for an exam and, meanwhile, to reconsider his spiritual values. I would have forgotten this meeting if I hadn't received a telephone call one month later requesting a visit. Jim had felt strange, painful disturbances for a long time and had foreseen possible disaster. He was a specialist in herbs and vitamins, and tried unsuccessfully to suppress his pain, thinking it insignificant. Jim, trusting his intuition, accepted the warning with an open mind and composure. During all of our therapy sessions, we never uttered the word "cancer". He avoided it, and I supported him in his efforts. It was his choice.

Before our sessions, we touched upon and discussed many topics. There were some issues we agreed on and some we disagreed on. Notwithstanding the differences in our approach to healing, he was scrupulous in carrying out my recommendations. As a nutritionist, Jim designed a diet for himself with a special set of vitamins and minerals, drank my "activated" water – water that absorbed energy from my palms – went to bed and awoke with prayer, carried out visual and breathing exercises that I advised and, continued his physical exercises. His combined efforts worked very well. His whole energy system was restored in a much shorter time than others. The old truths confirm themselves: the one who believes in healing, intuition, and the Natural laws wins in the struggle, as opposed to others who try to push them aside as something unreal and immaterial.

There is a subtle world that dictates its laws to us which we must not break but learn. We behave as silly, naughty children, thinking that we will be forgiven if we ask. Yet there is a major flaw in this idea. In one stage of life, it can be forgiven. But in the next generation or a future life, it might reverberate with new force. Every reckless step is recorded in the memory of the cosmic processor and enters into the law of Karma, which follows everyone. There is only a small possibility of lessening its effect and the question arises: At what cost? Everything is balanced in Nature and there is no vacuum. In order to reduce the effect of cosmic punishment, one must mobilize all spiritual and physical strength, and one is not always prepared for the battle.

Each time I encounter a new cancer patient, I become more convinced of the direct dependence of the cancer patient on his own and his relatives' psychologic stance. When medical staff conveys the message to the patient about the diagnosis of cancer, most patients instantly accept the inevitable. On the subconscious level, such mental orientation by itself is 99% responsible for the outcome. Therefore, I have to have a lengthy conversation with each potential oncology patient, carefully examining his mindset, will to live, and relatives' reactions, as well as his relationship with them. The result of such discussion in most cases is the return of faith in one's physical and psychological strength, leading to reconsideration of spiritual values and consequently, to victory over the disease. I remember cases in my practice when the patient's relatives did not support his wish to live, thereby consistently and purposefully destroying his endeavors and experiments in fighting the disease.

A young woman present at one of my lectures asked me several questions and took my business card. Anabel was surrounded by an unpleasant, cold energy field. A month later, I got a call asking for an appointment. Usually, before the visit, I conduct a distance diagnosis with the new patient; this patient manifested a slowly progressing cancer of the lymphatic system. Anabel told me during our first meeting that in my presence she felt at peace, something which had been long missing. That experience led her to consult me.

Beginning with our first session, Anabel felt such relief that her relatives began to wonder what was happening. She joked with pleasure about the change. Gradually, the lymphatic knots started to decrease in size. We could see her bloom. As her immune system gained in strength, her skin color changed. She was born again and a wish for changing her life developed. Feeling better, Anabel began making plans to relocate after she finished treatments. Suddenly one day, Anabel decided not to attend any more therapy sessions. During a telephone conversation, she mentioned that she could not finish, but could not tell me why. As it turned out later, her younger sister did not want things to change. I sometimes review the video interviews which Anabel gave before and after her sessions, trying to understand which counterargument presented by her family served as an obstacle to her healing. She moved to another state and I lost touch with her.

I think the impact of Karma is also manifested to some degree. Long-term debilitating diseases require willpower on the patient's part, which is depleted over time without support. If you don't accept what is happening right now, you revert to the past. You cannot perform a physical healing without cleansing the spiritual layers accumulated not only in the current lifetime but also in previous lives and generations. We create our karma by our thoughts and deeds.

I recalled Anabel's confession during our conversation about the interconnectedness of events, touching upon past incidents in which she had done regretful things to her brothers which she would not discuss. Her conscience still could not reconcile some bad deeds, but asking for spiritual and personal forgiveness never entered her mind. So, you see, dear friends and relatives – what unparalleled force and support – ready to save you – you carry! And how suddenly you are capable of destroying your dreams, your health. Stop and think before you try to alter the course of someone's life when they are seeking help.

The following case completely differs from the last one. Melissa was alone with her troubles, but she never lost her faith in Higher Forces. Melissa was a medical worker and smoked all of her life. One day on the job, she coughed up blood. After a full medical examination, including biopsy, she was diagnosed with lung cancer of the third stage. Furthermore, it was inoperable. Melissa quit smoking. According to official statistics, smoking is responsible for almost 90% of all lung cancer cases. As usual, chemotherapy and radiation therapy were prescribed by her physician. After a month, Melissa asked me for help. She came because of a faith in folk medicine cultivated in her childhood.

First, I advised Melissa to pray. Second, during the bioenergy-therapy, I recommended that she stop eating meat products. Simultaneously, she had to start breathing and visualization exercises according to my method. There is an unwritten law – to receive, you must ask. She began and finished each day with requests for total forgiveness.

In the first weeks of Melissa biotherapy, the pain in the lower part of her abdomen disappeared and it became easier for her to breathe. To her astonishment, the swelling in her legs that had been occurring for more than 20 year ceased completely. The drastic transformations shocked all of her relatives, who were prepared for the worst. Even though she had worked all her life in the medical field, Melissa's faithfully followed my recommendations. Melissa was a difficult patient because by nature she didn't trust people. There must be a particular psychological compatibility and mutual trust between the healer and the patient, especially in oncological problems.

During my work with each cancer patient, there arises a need to explore his or her personal life and the lives of his or her parents, including the lives of previous generations. Often the source of disease is not found in the place suspected by today's doctors, even if they search for it. In addition to all that was confided to me, I knew that Melissa, although married, did not have any children. I did not know why. I noticed that after each session, her energy seemed to stay with me in the room. It seemed that Melissa had decided to continuously keep me and the session in her mind, explaining that she felt relieved. I asked her to terminate this preoccupation and to choose something more interesting, like drawing. The patient cannot spend all his or her free time in thought about the disease. Enjoyment of life is a more certain way toward recovery.

The ability to renounce gloomy and sad thoughts brings more success in healing than constant self-flagellation. Positive emotions play an invaluable part in accelerating the recovery process, augmenting the activity of the immune system. One cannot always deny the world around oneself and frequent social activities. Being among friends and relatives, and attending cultural or sporting events give one freedom and rest, fulfilling defense functions at certain times.

For the first time in my experience, I perceived a specific feeling of discomfort during my first visit with Melissa at her home, which can be compared with being in a stuffy room. I cannot forget that experience. I simply could not breathe. It became clear that it was necessary to tell her about my sensations and refuse future services. But for some unknown reason, I instead advised her to move to another house or to at least clean her present house really well. Decades of negative energy had accumulated in her house, forcing me to leave the building. After sharing my feelings with Melissa, I felt that I could not leave her alone with the disease. Changing her place of residence in her condition and at the age of 63 was not feasible. Thus, Melissa did the following according to my recommendations. She cleansed the house of negative energy by using Epsom salts, keeping her windows open, and removing the old carpet. Changes appeared very soon. It was easier for me to breathe. Conditions were possibly helped by our having several healing sessions in the building, saturating it with positive energy.

At the same time, the chemotherapy and radiation therapy weakened Melissa's state of health. However, with the start of my therapy, an improvement in breathing occurred, pains in the small intestine disappeared, and her skin color began to change. Her cheeks acquired a rosy complexion. Her kidney functions improved and her appetite increased. In a month, her cough entirely disappeared. Keeping up with my recommendations, Melissa started each morning by visiting her church where she asked for forgiveness and release from negative information accumulated by previous generations that reflected on her. Her journal summary of the process of treatment after three months follows:

"This morning, Rachel gave me another treatment, and I must say that I am feeling better and stronger every day. Today, as my therapy progressed in the usual fashion, Rachel again extended her efforts to my chest and specifically to the area where my lung had been diseased. She placed one hand over the chest and extended her arm upward. I first experienced cold, then warmth again. Cold and warmth – thus alternating. Then I felt a new sensation that is difficult to describe. At first it felt comparable to a gentle tugging or pulling on the surface of my skin, but yet it seemed as if it had a slightly deeper origin than skin surface. Perhaps, a 'mild external suction' combined with a gentle presence from within may describe this sensation more accurately."

After several months, the sensations perceived by my palms changed. The strong pricking sensations transmitted to the inner surface of my palms at the location of tumors had weakened or disappeared. X-ray results after two months of working with Melissa confirmed that the first tumor left a trace of a scar. The second tumor, which was inoperable, had decreased to one-third of its size. This had a 2% chance of happening, as stated by the oncologist that treated her.

Over time, all the specific energy signals indicating the cancer cells had disappeared. Six weeks later, the next X-ray reflected no trace of a scar from the first tumor, while the second one had left a scar.

What had happened was quite expected from my point of view. My forecasts had become a reality. However, her doctor, working in a large hospital, did not have time to analyze the recovery process for this unusual patient. The physician continued to follow the designated routines, targeted towards an average patient. The unforeseen occurred. This doctor prescribed an additional course of chemotherapy, "to make sure," so to speak, even though the tumors were no longer there!

From the beginning of the new chemotherapy sequence, a wave of side effects was generated and not manifest during the bioenergetic sessions. It is no use to describe it all, as the negative consequences were kept at bay with my help. But why was another cycle of chemotherapy prescribed? Perhaps the physician felt he had nothing to lose by ordering more chemotherapy in that case, since the patient was doomed according to medical predictions. No one would blame the doctor for trying to save his patient's life.

The energy fields of the ailing body, stuffed with chemicals, create an invisible, elastic barrier for healing efforts. Everyone who does healing with the aid of Higher Forces knows this. Nature does not permit intervention from the outside in the form of unnatural chemical substances. That is why I ask a new client during our first visit if he takes any medications and which ones, in order to know what surprises might be waiting for me. I don't have any moral right to rescind or forbid the medication, as it is not in my competence and power legally. Perhaps we find comfort through traditional medicine. In coming to a doctor's office, we forget that we are dealing with our own health and that we are responsible for it. No one else knows better which problems truly exist and arise inside our own bodies. I would like to note that when edema of Melissa's lungs started, absent during the main course of treatment and appearing only after additional chemotherapy, a new biopsy was taken. The complete absence of cancer cells forced the doctor to discontinue the chemotherapy.

After that, more than one session was needed to eliminate the side effects. Melissa finally declared that if I helped her to get rid of lung cancer, it would be no effort for me to remove a small growth on her hand, which was unnoticeable. People sometimes forget that Nature is governed by its own laws. In the Russian folk tale "The Magic Gold Fish" by Alexander S. Pushkin, a fisherman was given magic wishes to have whatever he wanted, but it was never enough for his wife! When his wife wished for power over the gold fish, everything changed back. Melissa's case is interesting because it reflects in pure form the major elements of emergence, culmination, and completion of the process of disease. It is never enough! It was never enough for Melissa! At that moment Melissa almost forgot about her miraculous recovery from the deadly disease.

I have rarely witnessed smiles on my patients' faces in the beginning of treatment – more often displeasure, ill-will, and, hidden in the depth of the soul, fear. The majority of patients share their problems and concerns with me, both past and current. By reviewing events that happened in their earlier years, it is sometimes possible to find the answer to the question: "Why did this happen to me?"

Some experiences of childhood or adolescence forever change the destiny of the patient, even if, in the depth of his own soul, he is trying to disregard them, not thinking they are the reason for his current problems. As we know, nothing passes without a trace. In one way or another, vulnerable spots of the defense system eventually yield to the stress of hidden events. By knowing where he experienced trauma in the past, the patient can re-create in his imagination all the events and close the gaps.

For example, take a young man named Ram, suffering from a faulty metabolism. When we investigated his past, we discovered that in a childhood summer camp, he was bullied by older children who often took away his food, leaving him hungry. We were trying to visualize the events of those days. As Ram said with humor: "I simply took pity on them in my imagination now and voluntarily offered my food to them since they were so hungry."

The events of the past, especially childhood, do not vanish without a trace. Parents are encouraged to cherish their children and treat them with great love and respect. In talking with people, we have discovered the long-forgotten traumas of childhood covered with layers of time are still within. The unparalleled significance of those traumas can be seen in oncology cases also.

Look into the depth of your memory, for there is some probability that you may find answers to what caused diseases and problems that may appear later in life.

The recollections of past childhood memories still hold Kara in a trap. It takes great courage for her to share her remembrances at times. Even to listen to such confessions is often difficult. The struggle which she had to endure is only known to the two of us. Winning over cancer in such cases is only possible by liberating the soul from the bitterness of childhood memories.

Kara wrote: "When I was six, my mother had a miscarriage. I remember my dad and uncle carrying her out to the car in a blood-soaked blanket to take her to the hospital. I was to stay by the phone and wait for Grandma and take care of my brother and sisters – all younger than me. I awake every night at the same time as if it is happening again. Why did I start here? Because it depicts the stress of those years. Mom was barely 23 and had four children and lost the fifth. I was so upset at seeing this, and all that blood. My grandmother took me to visit my mother in the hospital. I remember this because Grandma frequently remarked that it must have been fate.

It was shortly after that visit that I was also hospitalized with pneumonia. I ached all over and it was difficult to explain to anyone what was wrong. I cried a lot, which only upset my parents; they had plenty of other things on their minds. My hospital confinement lasted more than three months, and when I was sent home, I was confined to bed for another six months. I was set apart from my brother and sisters.

I recall one most unusual night while in the hospital. My fever was quite high and I must have been delirious. I felt my body growing large and then small. My heart hurt tremendously, an experience I would not want to repeat. A young nurse's aide stayed with me throughout the night. She's the one, I believe, who thought I would not make it through the night. That's been almost 45 years ago. Yet I felt connected to something that happened that night... Mom and Dad were alcoholics and often, in my opinion, neglected the youngest kids. They loved them, but were overwhelmed with the adult events in their lives..."

In such situations, I recommend sitting alone for an evening with one's memories, a pen and a blank sheet of paper in front of a candle, a big ashtray and matches. Write down on the paper all that haunts you, read it only once, and burn it with a pure heart. Picture in your imagination that, by burying the ashes of the reminiscences oppressing your soul, you are reborn, cleansed from all causes that led you to your current life situation. Try it, and you will feel an inner relief. Your visualized victory over yourself will soon be fruitful in the victory over your ailment.

I saw the newly-produced relief first-hand on the face of one patient who wrote out her haunting memories and burned them from her heart over the candle's flame.

Oncologic problems do not arise during one month or year; years have to pass. Sometimes they are only revealed by autopsy after death.

Margo had swelling of her legs at age 14. Since then, Margo had never seen them in a normal condition until I started treating her. What had caused it? What was her secret? It took almost 50 years to make the hidden apparent. Indeed, Margo had started to secretly smoke at age 14, even though it was forbidden. Margo was in the medical profession.

Or, maybe this mystery unraveled after one of her patients, suffering from lung cancer, started to cough at her, not covering her mouth. The unrestrained behavior of the sick woman shocked Margo. In the next two months, she was diagnosed with the same problem. How striking this incident must have been, that it was fixed in Margo's memory!

I wouldn't have paid any attention to her swollen legs, if another cancer patient, Dr. Ellen, listening to the recording of an anonymous interview, had not immediately connected the two cases separated by time. Ellen asked me: "When, in your opinion, did her situation develop?" Without thinking, I replied not earlier than five years ago, which she confirmed for herself with a particular recollection. The information helped her find the source of her problem. It is always quite interesting to treat doctors, especially if they are involved in research, because I can exchange experiences and knowledge.

The above relationship between leg swelling and the future manifestations of a specific condition reminds me of another case from my practice. A 40-year old, vigorous woman, Toni, came to me with a series of health problems which the doctors were trying to eliminate by various medications. The process evoked a burst of side effects, until the doctors, exhausted by uncertainty, told her that she must have an allergy to one of the chemicals. One piece of evidence for the doctors was the swelling of her legs, a fact she shared during her first visit.

I want to add that this was told to me only during her first visit. During the distance scan, before I met her in person, I had set a diagnosis: the initial stage of lung cancer. The diagnosis was verified during my examination of her outer energy field – familiar, unpleasant signals.

During the first session, Toni perceived instantly the pain in her lungs. My first non-negotiable recommendations to her were to quit smoking immediately and see an oncologist before beginning regular therapy sessions with me. Below is her reaction to the news and the sensations she experienced.

"How I felt after my first treatment – I felt scared, confused, yet calm and determined to find the answer to correcting the imbalance in my body. It is a shock to the system to be told you have cancer in the right lung, especially with no physical proof other than a fear deep inside – it's true. The treatment of healing therapy was relaxing and soothing to the body. I felt pain and a cold, indescribable sensation in my lungs. I left feeling calm and serene."

She was not the first in her family to suffer from this condition. It is difficult and often impossible for some to realize that disease is not far away and that, actually, they are already sick. Nobody and nothing, except gifted healers and the patient himself, know prior to the approach of disaster. Sometimes it is too early for the doctor to diagnose a health problem. Then healers and close relatives and friends are there to support the patient in his struggle for life. The decision about the continuation of life itself depends only on the individual.

Because each patient is different, the body reacts differently to the healing energy. Sometimes it is even difficult for the healer to analyze how the process will work. On one hand, each disease develops according to its laws. The causes of cancer vary from patient to patient. Therefore, each time one has to deal with new factors from a patient's history in order for recovery to accelerate. For the patient himself, the knowledge of the beginning of the disease allows restructuring the whole existential system of world view, both spiritually and materially. The combined efforts of the healer and the patient pave the road to knowledge and to self-healing of the enfeebled body.

Due to the special relationship established between the healer and the patient during their sessions, the particles of consciousness of the patient are updated, restructured, and returned to the patient as one's new world outlook, destined to prevent serious disorder in the future.

One cannot be healed without changing one's inner self. The healer's part in such situations resembles the role of the teacher to the student, and his/her significance is invaluable. To be successfully healed, the patient and healer must work as a team. It is like dancing with a partner; the steps are performed in unison. Skillfully directing the thirst for knowledge, the healer attentively watches the spiritual growth and physical recovery of the patient until the patient has enough strength for the next step, the transition to independence. The right information and the truth about yourself allow you to take full responsibility for your health and life choices.

Every disease, especially cancer, can be dealt with from two points of view. First, the possessor of the body is given a warning that it is time to reconsider life events in order to make a timely readjustment of his views and attitudes toward the challenges of his surrounding world. Second, time in the diseased state does not pass unproductively. In the days and months of suffering, the sick person, by accumulating an enormous amount of information from different sources, can perceive the action of one of the main laws of philosophy: the law of transition of quantity into quality. The process of developing awareness of one's disease leads to recuperation with the help of a doctor or a healer and with one's own aid as well, through one's subconscious.

In our age, time is so saturated with activity that there is not sufficient attention to self-knowledge, self-control, and analysis of the health of one's own body while there is still time to restore the broken balance and take preventive measures.

Why do we react only to pain? The pain tells us that it is time to visit the doctor, but in reality it is a delayed reaction to the disorders in our body which we neglected earlier in our life. There is a good expression: "Pain is the guard dog of our health."

From my long experiences with diseases caused by karma's manifestations, a certain rule becomes clear. Over many years, our close relatives, friends, and even we ourselves begin to notice some marked aberrations in behavior: a strong reaction to some unimportant event, changes in voice, an irritability, or need for support in deciding even insignificant issues, etc. While searching for the solution to the situation, we rush around looking for those who can give us advice, ignoring that the best counselor is our self and our subconscious, which knows everything.

Finally, when we have become physically and psychologically weakened, with advice from our friends, we can end up with a psychiatrist. In olden days, the role of counselor belonged to the elders in any group or to the spiritual authorities of all religions.

In the next case, the victim of self-deception was Dr. Jean, nearly 40-years old, who experienced complications in her close relationships. Because this problem was never resolved in her consultations with her psychologist, her trusted friend brought Jean to meet me.

I diagnosed cancer in her ovaries. This had provoked her unusual behavior toward people around her and changes in her liver. Jean left the office confounded and confused, under the condition that she would return only after the confirmation of the diagnosis by traditional medicine.

A year passed before she called requesting an appointment. Before Jean came for consultation, I did a distance scan that verified the diagnosis given a year ago, but in a more advanced stage – ovarian cancer of the third stage. At the time of her visit, the woman's menstrual cycles had stopped. She hadn't yet even started thinking about children. She also had bloody discharges from her vagina. Jean had gone through all kinds of laboratory tests and exams that revealed nothing, but the results did not allay her fears. In addition, she had visited three other healers. She finally returned to me, accepting the original diagnosis. But time had not waited and was continuing its job.

After each session, we discussed the course of the therapy and analyzed historical factors in connection to her disorder. Some of those discussions made her search for answers, remembering moments which had once impacted her psychologically. One of them happened during her medical residency at a cancer center, where Jean had attended to a beautiful, young woman with ovarian cancer, the wife of a diplomat. The state of this woman had affected Jean emotionally, as did the condition of similar patients for whom she was caring.

A patient does not tell the doctor all of the information coherently. It is often extracted in parts. Jean once asked me when the first symptoms of her disease had emerged, to which I replied not earlier than ten years ago. Mentally considering the time frame, Jean affirmed what I had said. She recalled that, ten years ago, she had suffered badly from influenza which weakened her immune system. The beginning of the search for the cause of the disease was set. Additional secrets were stored in genetic memory.

How much time had been lost while her psychologist analyzed her actions? Yet it was not so difficult for me to diagnose her problem. A weakened immune system can rarely stand alone in the struggle with cancer. We simultaneously performed the investigations – she from the position of the patient/doctor and I – from the healer's point of view. What lurks behind the disease? How and why is a certain person, and not another, prone to cancer? What connection exists between different aspects of the life of the given patient, including the past and the present? If permission from above is provided, what aid can be offered to the afflicted to restore his normal activity?

Jean's journaled confession, given to me after the completion of therapy, deserves attention from the perspective of the psychological perception of the second healing session. "Today is the second healing session from an ovarian cancer that Rachel found yesterday. We had a long chat during the previous session. Many different topics of healing, energy, and protection were touched. At the beginning of this session, when I was lying on the table and Rachel was working, I felt an intense cold sensation. I was trembling. After being covered, the coldness persisted. During this time, I was trying to visualize a blue light as a scan-laser working through my ovaries. First I did the right ovary; I sensed it was a problem. When I did the visualization in the left, I sensed it was in more trouble, and I scanned it with blue light and it was left as a honeycomb. I also had the sensation that there was distortion of the left fallopian tube. After this visualization, which coincided with the moment Rachel was placing her hands on the back and top of my abdomen, I sensed that the ovary and the tube were fully repaired. I also had three images coming: first, as if Rachel were a Virgin Mary with a baby in her arms, very tall; second, there was an Indian or Egyptian man; and the third was a young woman wearing a white top and pink shorts, balancing in acrobatic sets. I also sensed the feeling of having with me two different male energies. At the end, I sensed a warm, vibrating energy covering me. I felt more relaxed and lighter."

The next example is not connected with oncology. Nevertheless, it is very convincing in another aspect. In talking with a 23-year-old man, Ted, about the depression and the various obsessive thoughts that had been pursuing him, I noticed an unnatural skin color for his age. It was not lifelike: it was pale gray color. I offered to diagnose him.

The testing of his aura showed clear deviation from normal function in energy centers that affirmed my suspicion: the presence of cranial trauma. From questions about early incidents that he remembered most, I had found out that indeed while playing baseball between eight and ten years of age, Ted got hit by a bat, after which he was taken to a hospital. Ted was surprised that he recalled that episode, considering it an insignificant event of long-gone childhood. However, ever since that event, it has been hard for him to remember school material and he has had severe headaches.

A drastic alteration in vibration of the field in the back of the head pointed out the location of trauma. Many strong, pain-suppressing medications had been prescribed over his life. He had edifying and harrowing conversations with psychologists, which made him shiver in recollection. Nobody thought it necessary to spend the time to dig into the real cause of all his problems. He only needed to have an X-ray and an encephalogram of the brain. The presence of an edema formed by damage to the head had led to numerous consequences in this young man's life.

I mention this incident so that the reader may devote greater attention to the analysis of his past when facing a problem either in health or in the state of mind. All of our problems stem from the past. Your best counselor and assistant is you, yourself, and only you. Before you decide to consult a psychiatrist, have a complete medical exam. If nothing wrong is found, maybe it's worth your while to look for a healer. Talk with trusted friends – do not use advertisements –to find a healer with a natural gift, one who is capable of establishing the hidden cause of your problem before it becomes apparent. We will many times touch upon the interrelationship of the past with the present, affecting the future.

More than once, I have faced a feeling of watchfulness and curiosity during my first encounter with a certain type of patient. Such people stand out by their manner or behavior, their facial expression, and the deep sadness in their eyes, together with the subtle changes in the energy field. The souls of such people, through the eyes and the body, manifest an unbearable despondency, a cry of despair, and a call for help. All of this happens on the subconscious level, as nothing has been yet manifested that affects the physical level. This plea arouses in me an impulsive compassion towards the patient. I mentally pose a question inside: "Does the person to whom I am talking know what's awaiting him in the future?" If the answer is affirmative, I try to establish a relationship with this person. Over time and if I feel it is necessary, during one of our conversations, I advise the person to see a physician for an examination. Whether the person heeds my suggestion is his choice. If the disease is not yet diagnosable by physicians, there is still benefit to seeing a good healer.

It is not easy to be a "scanning device" for the invisible diseases of people encountered in social settings or business meetings. I remember one such episode. At an official reception, while talking to one of my acquaintances, I blurted out something about my gifts and slightly lowered my hand down, telling him that he should visit a doctor. I told him this only out of compassion, as the illness was already written on his face. The motion of the hand was only to confirm the truth of my statement through energy scan. At the next meeting, Darryl said that his doctor could not find anything. I insisted that he visit a specialist. In a few months, I was informed that I was right. I did not offer my help. He already had sufficient information to make a correct decision. Since Darryl was uncomfortable that I knew his secret health problem, he chose to avoid me.

Once when I saw my old acquaintance, Harry, I sensed that something unusual was affecting his health. The mental diagnosis suggested stomach cancer of the second stage, although a slightly dry cough masked it as a possible problem dealing with the lungs. What should one do in such a case? To tell or not to tell? Will he take it seriously or bar himself from such news? Intuitively, I didn't utter a word, thinking that he would lack the courage and willpower to confront the shocking discovery, and fight the disease. He does not have a family or children, and I have often wondered about the history of his family. Let him spend the remainder of his life peacefully, being satisfied with contacts in the sphere of his friends and colleagues. After making this decision, I felt released from a heavy burden.

I often ask myself the question, why I am not ordained to convey comforting or encouraging news to all those in need? Who is behind all that? Why is everything not in our power? Who decides what is allowed to us, and what is not?

In case after case, new details about the onset of the disease and the recovery of the patient came to the surface. How did it start? How is it developing? What is the lesson to be learned from the disease? In every situation, the mindset of the patient regarding the will to fight the ailment comes first, not the wishes of his family. Whether it is nervous or physical, and no matter whether it occurs on an earthly or cosmic level, the presence of the spirit in the battle for life is critical. Each patient is an individual, although the causes of diseases similar to cancer coincide. Therefore, the roads that guide us to deliverance are often similar. At the same time, the details vary because of different circumstances and the peculiarities of patients' characteristics. It is the patient's choice to decide whether to fight for life.

Chapter IV

THE INVISIBLE
REALITY

Every answer given arouses new questions.
The progress of science is matched by an
increase in the hidden and mysterious.
                                    —Leo Baeck

Mystics always hope that science will
some day overtake them.
                                —Booth Tarkington

For a long time I couldn't write about this forbidden topic, thinking I would be misunderstood, or censured and it might arouse unpleasant emotions in my past, present, and future patients as well as in me. However, the desire to share my experience prevailed over the fears, even beyond warnings from my friends and relatives. All that appears physically unreal at the present moment or that is currently shamefully concealed may tomorrow prove to be quite a normal phenomenon, leaving no one in distress. I hope that someone finds my extensive experience and accumulated knowledge useful while searching for answers to their doubts, or that it helps in their struggle with their own or another's imminent ailment.

This chapter is devoted to those invisible phenomena, beings and realities that surround and accompany every mortal substance on our planet Earth. They are our reflections, instructors, friends, advisors, and helpers. It is those from the so-called "unreal" world who come to help us in our most critical hour when it seems everything else has failed. In different cultures and faiths, this "unreality" is termed the other side, the mirror reflection, or the world of the dead, angels, spirits, etc. I prefer to call it the **Quasiworld**.

The **Quasiworld** is that loftier reality that exists independent of our world, and to which state our soul has aspired since the most ancient ages. The exchange of information between these two interconnected and peacefully coexisting realities is a constant dynamic of invisible processes.

When I was thinking about how to explain the transmission of information between the material world and the invisible Quasiworld, I was given the word "Hent." I grasped that this term is a cosmic universal particle that passes between different dimensions. In my understanding of this exchange, I envision an energetic messenger named "**Hent.**"

"**Hent**" is my hypothetical term for the indivisible and unchanging particle, equivalent to the neutrino, carrying an intellectual message between ordinary reality and the Quasiworld. Hent is a material, informational particle, not yet measured by existing methods, that is the conveyor of that intelligence and information reaching us through many paths: dreams, sensations, intuition, and reason, as a result of our investigations through divination or during our indirect connections to the cosmic data bank or collective consciousness.

The ways of acquiring needed information from the Quasiworld are numerous. Sometimes we receive this information through meditation, sometimes we sense it intuitively, and other times we receive messages in our dreams. Everybody has their own way of receiving this knowledge. However, having a respectful attitude toward the information supplied by the Quasiworld brings beneficial outcomes. With this knowledge, one can take appropriate measures to prevent the development of disease, to diminish a pending stressful situation, or even to alter unpleasant situations by choosing the correct solution.

Every creature on earth has its own quasi-companions or guardians. They are the unseen ones who can prevent undesirable or tragic results. Let us remember how our ancestors treated the spirits with reverence, appeasing them ritually with sacrifices, prayers, and many other ceremonies that have sunk into oblivion over the ages. A number of these rites were sketched on the interior walls of caves, or in Egyptian pyramids, on obelisks, and temples or monuments of Incas, Aztecs, Mayans, and many other cultures of the ancient world.

For example, one of the African tribes of pygmies still maintains that we are governed by the world of the dead. Ancient Egyptians believed the same. We, with our modern views, would be considered heretics by them. Who is right? Human experience will show over time that it is impossible to simply divorce these ancient ideas from our historical development. We are reluctant to acknowledge these concepts as reality because not everybody has had this experience. Only some people, endowed from birth or, from the result of a tragic situation, such as an accident or illness, now have spirit sensitivity, are able to use their special gift to see the presence of quasi-beings and are capable to sense the existence of **Quasi-forces** in this world. It is not easy to forget the awe in being aware of the existence of invisible phenomena, a side effect perhaps of the fires of the Inquisition, resulting in fear of the unknown or fear of change.

Only the polytheistic religions treat the subtle realms with reverent worship. In "modern" opinion, people from the "third world" countries place too much significance on invisible forces. Although those who live in civilized countries perceive ourselves as conquerors of Nature, those from third world countries believe we still roam in darkness searching for truth. When Reality is placed in front of us, we do not wish to see it, afraid to confront the truly powerful forces of this world. We are not the creators of these forces, only a part of them, and we cannot survive without them.

Quasiworld was included only to show the central role it has played in my daily work and practice. I am convinced that it is also present in your life. It is quite possible that after reading this chapter, you will reevaluate some past events from your own experience. I have no doubt that every person has something to tell, if not to his children, and then at least to his grandchildren, who, with eager enthusiasm, will grasp his words with full trust.

As adults, we stifle the desire in our children to share their discoveries, laughing at their fantasies and mocking their stories in our conversations with other adults. Parents should listen more closely to their children's stories and not immediately assume that a visit to a doctor for medication is needed. To protect their privacy, parents should be wary of sharing their children's visions with just anyone. As the child grows up, he either forgets his visions or keeps them to himself. As an adult, those who are creative such as an artist, writer, musician or other professional shares the products of this secret world view through expression. It is shaped into words, paintings, or sounds, fulfilling the cultivated emotion and impressions. In this form, nobody will consider it an insanity or will dare to debase the object of art. Seeking confirmation of hidden knowledge, some find themselves attracted to those creative works that reflect their private, inner world. It helps those people recognize that they are not alone in their thoughts and feelings. The rest keep their subtle secrets.

From folk tales to written accounts, there is much information about contacts and experiences with Quasiworld or the "other side" as it is called by some. Like most people, I find it exciting to share these mysterious moments of my life and to tell about the "unusual" phenomena encountered by my relatives, acquaintances, and patients.

Let me start with powerful moments embedded in my memory. By the will of fate, I was thrice saved from almost certain death: once during a voyage, another time while walking through the Caspian mountains, and again in a seemingly inescapable automobile accident when the steering wheel turned in the right direction by itself, without visible help. I learned when a tragic moment was supposed to happen to me, I never thought about myself. In each instance, I only thought about my closest ones and how they would survive without me. And at that dreadful flash, a miracle saved my life more than once.

Once my son was frightened by a mysterious spirit sitting in the corner of his bedroom, gazing at him. My son described the ghostly visitor in a trembling voice and I told him, "This is your protector; do not be afraid of him." These strange occasions are numerous in our memories. One has only to think of past events to remember.

As I grew up in Belarus, a non-religious nation of the former Soviet Union, I had a normal family life. I never gave a thought to the existence of quasi-creatures. Trusting only my instincts, I vaguely sensed someone or something was in charge of me. In dangerous situations when there seemed no relief or no reason to hope for help, a little miracle occurred.

What role indeed does this not-quite-visible Quasiworld with its invisible inhabitants play in the art of healing? I will share some of my mystical experiences. I will also include some experiences from patients who were not afraid to share their perceptions and insights with me.

During one journey to Russia, my travel mate noted, in passing, "You have an angel behind your back which not only protects you but your whole family." This long-awaited confirmation of what I cherished most led me to search for the name of that quasi-entity. In our society, everything has a name or title. Everything is classified and put on its shelf.

Some months after returning from my trip, I happened to be in the Theosophical Society's library in Wheaton where my attention was drawn to the book compiled by Dora Kunz called *Spiritual Healing*. I checked out the book. To my delight, I came across on insightful article by Dr. Bernie Segal, "Spiritual Aspects of the Healing Arts". After reading the article in which he mentioned how he meditated to discover the name of his invisible companion, I attended one of his seminars. During intermission, I asked Dr. Segal how he had learned the name of his spiritual guide. He said he couldn't explain it by logic because it was an intuitive process. Later, I came to realize that everyone has his/her unique experiences becoming introduced to his/her guides.

Because I went to the seminar specifically to find the name of my quasi-friend, I was disappointed. During the break I mentally tried out names to give to my invisible friend. However, I could not find a proper name. Quite unexpectedly, his name entered my consciousness – the name came naturally even though I had never before heard the name. I liked it immediately. The name came to me because he was a quasi-entity. As I found out later, the quasi-entities do not differ by names or gender, but the name was given so that I could communicate with my friend.

My quasi-friend seemed to be of Italian origin and lived in Italy one thousand years ago in our material dimension. He is 22 or 24 years old, with curly, black hair, and he wears a cap with a feather in it.

To help humans as spiritual guides, our quasi-friends have to earn the right through positive incarnations. From then on, it was easier to communicate with him and his friends. They often arrived in the midst of complicated situations with a given patient. Other times, the quasi-specialists would arrive earlier, as if waiting for their own sick patient.

At first, I often relied on my quasi-friend consultations. But, as I became more comfortable with my own knowledge, I sometimes overlooked his suggestions to my peril. For instance, he advised me against working with a particular person. Whenever I ignored his advice, I had problems. I disregarded his advice in the case of a woman in her late thirties, who was recommended to me because she was experiencing severe pain in her head. Ignoring my quasi-friend, I went ahead and conducted several sessions with her. Not only did she discontinue my treatments, but also she neglected to pay me for the healing I had performed.

Once after reading a book describing treating patients by hypnosis where deceased physicians and healers from past centuries entered the body of the living healer, I decided to try it myself. At that time, a friend suggested that I grant permission for the quasi-substance to enter my body during the therapy session for curative purposes, thank it, and then release it. In exchange, should the quasi-specialists need my knowledge, I give them permission to tap into my DNA. When the quasi-specialists need me, I feel the overwhelming need to rest, sometimes for a few minutes, sometimes longer. I don't remember exactly what happens, but afterwards I awake with a sense of fulfillment.

The first infusion of quasi-energy within my body left a distinct memory. The sensations of the patient are described further on. In the middle of one of my curative sessions with a woman afflicted with cancer, I stepped forward to conduct an unforgettable experiment. Concentrating deeply, I asked my quasi-friend to please help me. A miracle happened! My hands were raised into the air without my assistance, as though suspended in weightlessness, and started contriving some elaborate movements and techniques without much meaning to me at the time.

From then on, the process of treatment not only became easier, but accelerated as well. Now before beginning treatment on the physical level, we restore the layer of the astral body. This is necessary because we must repair holes in this layer created by negative energy. Every quasi-assistant is endowed with his own manipulations and movements, peculiar only to him and not to be mixed with others' methods.

By studying these unusual body and hand movements, I now understand their purpose. Still, there is much to learn and I receive something new with each patient. It requires a huge effort to duplicate these movements on my own, much more difficult than when combined work with my quasi-assistants. Therefore, I never use those motions independently of them.

In time, not only my quasi-friend utilized my hands, but other quasi-doctors also came to my aid. This was discovered when the hand manipulations began to alter from patient to patient. New specialists and new names of invisible assistants appeared. Each of them was endowed with or was expert in a particular experience, temperament, charm, or energetic background. Besides that, each quasi-specialist had a preference toward the background music played during the sessions!

To repeat the actions of invisible forces is not feasible for me, but may be for others who wish to reproduce them. Composer Shostakovich would not have been able to re-create his emotional experience, were he to attempt to compose anew the "Leningrad Symphony." This is a truth found in many languages: "You cannot enter the same water of river twice." Only through individual compassion for human suffering is one given a mandate from above to cure, and the blessing to employ special devices and the forces of the impalpable world, with which the Creator of the Universe furnishes us when the need arises.

That first unforgettable experience of working with the quasi-forces is well illustrated by Jenny, one of my patients. During a session with her, I asked my quasi-friend for help because of the seriousness of her condition. Jenny said, "In my pancreas, I perceived the sensation of bulging air bubbles, ready to ascend, erupting through a volcano. I became aware of a vigorous push, resembling the eruption of the volcano, with a simultaneous feeling of physical pressure in the area of the transverse intestine. There appeared to emerge material forms, connecting something physically intangible for me, at the pancreas, with the perception of some movement in the intestine, like a stream of gas during fermentation. The sensation of a gentle, cool breeze enveloping my whole body remained during the session, as well as currents of warm waves, rolling across my back, reminding me of high and low tides. The perception of the material contact of the palms in the solar plexus, or their motion above the forehead, during those moments when Rachel's location had changed, was different. I have double-checked several times, doubting the reality of what was happening . . ."

Because Jenny awoke under the influence of our invisible companions, her explanation of her sensations was somewhat disorganized. Jenny was gifted with an unusually strong energy field. As a rule, such patients have more problems because they ignore the early warnings of negative body signals.

What can then be said about the majority of people who have a normal energy field? I receive many lessons of love toward life and people, thanks to my patients who willingly reveal their emotions! I am grateful they trusted me with the feelings and sensations they perceived during the sessions. They help me to realize that much still needs to be learned. Not everyone is allowed to experience such indescribable sensations. Experiences depend on differences in psychological belief about reality, on the structure of the energy bodies surrounding the physical organism, on the degree of access with the cosmic information fields, on specific inherent gifts, on the uniqueness of interpersonal relationships between the healer and the patient, and on the presence of special quasi-substances accompanying the living entity from the moment of birth. As imperfect humans, we cannot explain everything.

During therapy directed on the astral level, my patients perceived new sensations from the moment quasi-specialists began to work. By chance, I learned that my patients could "see" this Quasiworld or other side during the treatment sessions. During one conference where I demonstrated the art of healing, Shelly was the first patient who described very simply and naturally, as though it were something ordinary: "I saw a young man standing aside and observing the treatment."

We often receive perceptions of the Quasiworld in images familiar to our feelings. Otherwise we would think all we have seen and heard is hallucination. Shelly perceived that image as a part of her reality, which did not frighten, shock, or scare her away. Her calm recognition of this parallel world – invisible under normal conditions to most people – is what urged me to pay more attention to my patients' stories that followed our bio-energy sessions. I'll share some of my patients' experiences and observations.

Polly came to see me because of gynecological problems. One of her stories is interesting because it is similar to stories from other patients: "I see a large surgical hall for students with a glass ceiling. I am lying on the table with a dissected body under bright lamps and see Rachel operating. Her actions are observed through the windows above by a group of five or six bald men in black suits and dark ties. She is assisted by, or in collaboration with, my quasi-friend and his helpers. The students from above, gazing at the course of the operation, continue with their study, coming from former lives, and are linked with Rachel in the present time. The ties are established between them on the subconscious level and are uncontrolled by their volition. The uninterrupted learning from an expert does not have any temporal or distance limits."

The above-mentioned session occurred during a thunderstorm. In thunderstorms, both electro and magnetic energies are present. I would not have paid any attention to the thunderstorm, except that, after the session, Polly's condition drastically improved. Since then, sometimes I recommend that certain patients, should they have a chance, arrange their sessions during thunderstorms or heavy rains. The enhanced effectiveness of such sessions has been verified many times by my patients. It is possible that, during such times, the patient finds it easier to sense the Quasiworld, the body reacts to the intensity of the session, and different quasi-specialists appear because a cosmic channel is opened especially for them, and they would not otherwise come.

Several years later, another patient described the treatment in the same words. In fact, Mel was able to sketch the invisible pupils (Fig. 4-1).

I have noticed that the presence of certain specific quasi-specialists lead to visible reactions in my clients. Those reactions included laughter, tears, vibration of extremities, visual perceptions, a sense of peace or blissfulness, and a state of trance. In this deep state, one no longer perceives the boundary between reality and the invisible realm.

We have to accept with an open mind everything naturally just as the information is presented. No matter what, the Quasiworld will not change its attitude toward us. We are only much-studied subjects for the Quasiworld entities who control and preserve order in our boundless Universe.

Pam, who was under my treatment due to cancer of the rectum, was embraced by the feeling of indescribable peace and tranquility while seeing an old, bearded face. The face had caring and understanding eyes. A voice said, "All that is hard is behind you." One image had no meaning for her – the eye that appeared somewhat later in the session and glowered at her with its tenacious gaze (Fig. 4-2).

"On my ribcage I felt how somebody took up and drew out the breeze from the left and center above my chest. This was painless, like the removal of stuck grass from my clothes after a walk in the park. I felt in my throat and head how she [Rachel] worked with them. I breathed deeply and openly. I felt a snap above my left eye and a cold touch during the treatment of my right buttock. When she touched 15 cm above my anus, I perceived a burning line of 8 cm in length, as if the left wall of the intestine was nipped below that area. During the session, my brain activity didn't stop producing thoughts and colors. Very small images were carried into the field of vision, but I couldn't hold onto them, colored crystals or a natural stone – a tiny figure, resembling a very beautiful doll. The colors, mostly dark red, blue and purple, rushed quickly through my mind. Thoughts concerning my grandmothers – I don't know why – came to me during the session, although I am sure they are connected with me by the process of treatment ..."

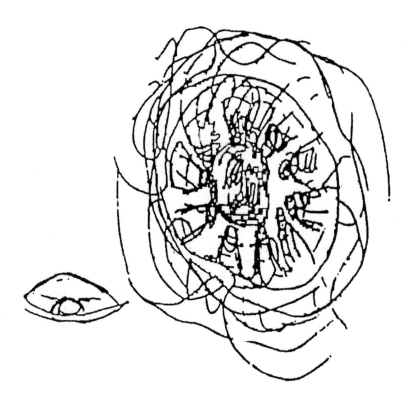

Fig. 4-1

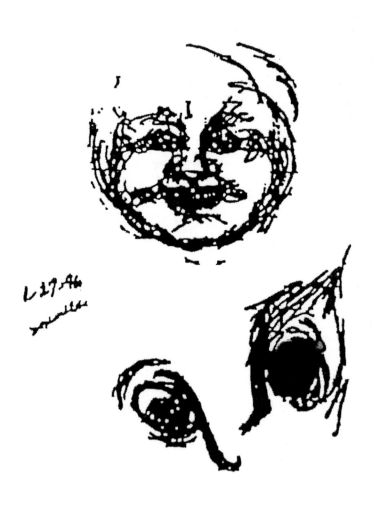

Fig. 4-2

The next case is somewhat different. A young woman, Nancy, consulted me at the right time. After only a few sessions, the energy level of Nancy's body was restored. Her world-view and sense of life completely changed. Here are her reflections, shared after one of the sessions. She originally sketched a picture of the reality she had seen.

"Two months ago my life seemed empty, boring. I have recently faced failure and trouble, which caused me pain and despair. It seemed to me that the entire world had turned upside down, and all that filled my life before became unreal, hopeless, and empty. After meeting you [Rachel], I felt a sort of lightness and a small hope that everything will be well and become right again.

"I remember how I sat opposite you and I couldn't talk very long, as my ears were getting terribly clogged up. I felt a pain in my neck, spine and stomach. During your work, I sensed warmth, force, actually a large force, as though about 10 people were working with me. When I tried to relax and slightly closed my eyes, after a little while I started to see gray protruding bodies like cocoons, with egg-shaped extended heads, having big slanting eyes. There were many of them, and they surrounded the table. At the time, when I started telling you [Rachel] that I can see them, they suddenly started to disappear, and I felt that the work began to cease. I closed my eyes so that I wouldn't interfere with my 'friends' treating me. During your 'operation,' I saw how they were throwing out of my opened body multi-colored energetic balls, and returned part of them, purified of something. I saw some kind of lightning which fell on me from above, and other small forms resembling 'butterflies,' escaping out of me. About the end of your session, I noticed how from above, on the side of my feet, the figures passed a little torchlight through all my organs, checking if everything was all right. I also saw light directed on me from above, and someone was looking at me very intently (Fig. 4-3)."

Black-white shades were used in the drawing, the butterfly was golden, and silvery tones are employed in the picture. It is a peculiar reflection of the experience. Nancy is presently feeling well.

Fig. 4-3

The next case is that of a depressed young woman, Iris. Although I have heard pleas for such help many times, the sobbing voice on the telephone made me believe she would not come to me. However, at the end of our conversation, she made an appointment to see me. Not everyone has the willpower to visit me or to secure support from their own families in the search for salvation from an imminent disaster. We often are so preoccupied with ourselves that we do not pay attention to our relatives and friends. Here are Iris's observations and sketches after her therapy sessions.

"During my first visit to Rachel, I was in dismay, which is almost forgotten now; fear accompanied me day and night. Waking up in the morning, I felt unrested, jaded; the thoughts were digging about in my head, one gloomier than another. It was difficult for me. It seemed a virtually impossible job to make breakfast for my son. Stomach aches, burning and nausea.

"I arrived on one of those days when I couldn't cope with myself and was afraid to be alone with my fears. The first session I cried and laughed, felt the waves, persistent commotion in my stomach, spasms. I was convinced that the session wouldn't help, since I couldn't help myself. Rachel instilled me with a great trust and confidence that everything would be well.

"During the second session, there were spasms in my stomach, wavelike and warm, and I laughed without the tears. Visions like the fog with the outlines of shadows visited me, together with spherical objects and a green beam (Fig. 4-4).

"In the third session, there were quite new impressions, visions and sensations in the area of my head, the crown, and the back of the head. In my stomach some foreign body was rotating.

"For the fourth session, I was almost completely calm, dozed off with a feeling of comfort, and did not even feel the table on which I lay. At one moment I felt as though the threads were unwound from me and I revolved in the air. In my head there was nothingness, tranquility, and silence (Fig. 4-5). Before this session, I had dreamt of dawn. One sun ray was especially bright, orange.

"For the fifth and last session, there were no physical sensations, except for comfortable ones. Many times during the

Fig. 4-4

84

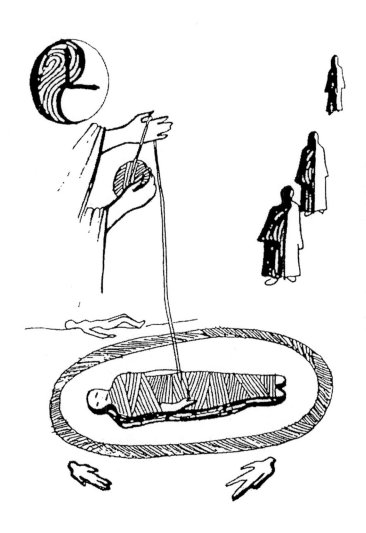

Fig. 4-5

sessions, there was a feeling of complete separation from the world and a feeling of flight, growing clouds, snowflakes flying, and a dance in the air, colors of blue-rosy hue (Fig. 4-6). Then, the sensation of an egg-shaped body surrounding mine, comprised of needles of light. I am immersed into a pulsating, glistening, rigid energy field (Fig. 4-7).

"I would like to thank Rachel, for she brought back to me the sensation of freedom, peace, even joy. Presently I have a feeling that someone is holding me from my customary reactions to what is happening around me, and I look on myself as though from the distance. The desire for physical movement has awakened inside of me. I do a lot of things around the house, and a yearning for a new life ahead is in me."

Being artistic in nature, Iris had the ability to express the witnessed quasi-reality more graphically in comparison to others with similar experiences.

The timely correction of aura surrounding the living leads to remarkable results, preventing the manifestation of organic deviations on the physical level. However, not everyone wishes to respond to signals arising from inside or outside. For some too busy pursuing their dreams, there is a perceived lack of time. The above description of quasi-substances was basically the same as that of another patient, Richard, whom I treated because of a cancerous disorder in the pancreas. During the session he could count 5 or 6 halos, resembling the above-mentioned figures, which surrounded him. Many of his impressions coincided with sensations experienced by my other clients, which brings me to some very interesting hypotheses.

We are surrounded by something that does not wish to be accessible to the senses of the majority. It makes me think that we live in the night vision of the world, where we can only observe those brightly illuminated objects to which we are permitted access. Actually, the larger reality only is revealed to a small number of select people. One must yet ponder carefully! Who studies whom? There is no explanation for the sudden appearance in several of my patients of similar visions of old faces with huge, handsome blue eyes attentively observing the healing process, as though giving assurance.

Fig. 4-6

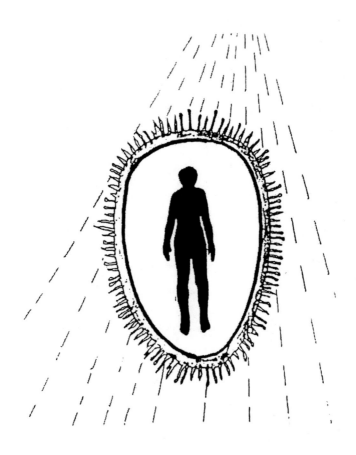

Fig. 4-7

How many people, with so many different perceptions, have perceived the actions of quasi-forces? Another example of visual manifestation of the actions of quasi-forces is depicted in the graphical re-creations of Barry. During his childhood, he lived under a very controlling environment, and only through coincidence thanks to his friends did he have the luck to release himself from the chains.

Let us begin with Barry's words: "I felt that my visit was predestined. I don't even know who could even understand me or help me. I know and sense that I am being worked on. I find myself as though in a cocoon of cobwebs, and they work as elves and I know that they are saying something, but I cannot express in words. What exactly is being done? Thousands of threads had entwined me, and skillful weavers had begun their job. The threads are gleaming with various colors which could be distinctly seen, as if when you pour gasoline on water, and during its movement, a magic glow emerges, taking a defined form. You [Rachel], by your actions, fashion those cocoon webs in that certain order which is destined for me at the given moment according to the blueprint – the undaunted director and conductor, Rachel. From the depth of my soul there rises a feeling, that you [Rachel] are the person who belongs to the highest selected circle. I felt anew my endlessly restless spirit, which started to acquire its place in my shell." The picture, drawn after the effect of the session, conveys those impressions (Fig. 4-8).

I encountered a phenomenon in which some patients are able to perceive unique scents exuded during the healing actions of quasi-substances or energy impacts. To some, they reawaken certain flower aromas. To others, they are connected to some pleasant memories. In those moments, the patients' faces always radiate blissful smiles.

In one of my sessions with Barry, he described his own experiences with quasi-forces. "I felt myself in such a relaxed state that there arose a sensation that I was Earth, enveloped by furry white clouds and peaceful stars. There was a sense of weightlessness. Suddenly, I found myself in the woods after the rain. The forest breathed out ozone, from which I became

Fig. 4-8

intoxicated. It is impossible to express simply this enveloping, inebriating feeling."

Another interesting occurrence is the sounds "heard" during sessions which, like the awarenesses above, are subtle and are not noticed in daily situations because we are earth-bound in our sensations. In the beginning of my regular sessions, I never paid much attention to reactions of patients to sound phenomena, but some of their vivid descriptions caused me to ponder.

During one of my healing meetings with Richard, I noticed how he seemed to be surprised, turning his head as though he distinguished something invisible moving around him. "You were working near my feet, when I heard distinct and confident masculine steps of the invisible man around me. Those sounds were so real that I looked around to find their source in the room, but no one except you and me were present. Several times I rechecked your location, doubting my senses."

Over time, I have incorporated visualizations of energy surgery with my patients, which became an integral component of the bio-therapy sessions. Knowing the anatomy and physiology of the human body, I visualize the flow of the operation dealing with an organ and picture it in my imagination. I also ask my quasi-colleagues to assist in the operation. In most cases, there are usually four or five such assistants, very rarely only one quasi-surgeon. The participants change, depending on the concrete case or situation.

One discovers interesting details. Even the Quasiworld possesses the same specializations as ours. In addition, they have a sort of hierarchy, which we poorly understand. Some beings are constantly participating in the operation on the particular patient, but others change from session to session, i.e., their presence is necessary for a specific procedure or technique. Sometimes, my quasi-colleagues are waiting in advance for their own patient yet to arrive, watching from above in their observation post over mankind. Others come for specific reasons, as though drawn by a connection during the process of an operation. They are perceived by patients visually and by psychic vision. Some patients are endowed with abilities to see and feel their actions, others are not. However, during complicated cases, all patients, without exception, unless they fear to become considered abnormal, describe material sensations which strike them during initial sessions. The perceived images of quasi-surgeons varying from human figures, described concretely in detail, to energy halos possessing the human, omniscient soul.

I recall one episode with Barry, who had a very serious problem. I saw with my closed eyes a surgical table surrounded by a group of people pulled from the darkness by a stream of light. Inside my soul, I understood that those were the quasi-beings who were conducting their manipulations over Barry at the given moment. Through intuition, I decided not to disturb them, lest the figure-visions vanish without a trace.

Working with the patient Pam, I discovered that during my visualization of the operation, she was also re-creating the healing process. According to her description, at one of the moments, we were both engaged in the same area where she herself had located a presence of danger and which I, as she reported, was systematically removing with white cold light. She sensed how dark brown bubbles, not belonging to that particular organ, were removed, becoming iridescent. Until that time, Pam was not aware of the reality of her disease, cervical cancer. For the first time, I heard how a patient described her sensations from the energy transmitted from the outside.

While sending bio-energy into the right side, the left side of Pam's body started to elicit "jealous" responses, which quite amazed Pam. She never expected that separate parts of her body could have such feelings and could communicate with each other.

In this way, I confirmed what was stated in eastern philosophy that each human body organ, is given independent intellectual potential and is capable of receiving commands and making decisions. Please, talk with your body and your organs, like with your best friends, if you perceive the approach of changes in your system.

The most colorful and picturesque sketch of a visual part of the operation was rendered by Lee. Each of my movements, each of my mental commands during the quasi-operation was instantly identified by her and repeated aloud, so that I could compare my actions with her responses during the analysis of therapy results. It is quite possible that this happened because, she was an artist familiar with anatomy, and it was easier for her to re-create in words the physically invisible actions of quasi-substances.

One of my patients made an interesting statement during a session. Barry said I belonged to a particular group of people whose responsibility from life to life was to heal. Afterwards, he asked me about my past lives. The question challenged me and put me at a dead-end. My patients, many times prior to this, had shared their impressions and mentioned the sensations they experienced. They sometimes described visions appearing to them during sessions in which my role during all ages was to heal people.

For unknown reasons, I had not connected my own, or my patients' destiny with past lives and their impact on today's events until Barry's question. This fact caught my attention since the quality of a past life could have influenced the state of health of my patients and the change in their karma. From then on, I started to analyze the emergence of disease in my patients, together with karmic influences from past lives, which helped me to secure better recommendations for their care.

I will never forget the feeling of burden and resistance to continuing the session with one amiable person, who was very much in need of help. During the therapy, he started to speak, as though matter-of-factly, about our past life together. He had once been my husband, who had not wanted to have children. The most astonishing fact was that, even in this life, he had lived 50 years and had never had any children, nor was he thinking about having them.

This and other facts linked several aspects of my accumulated information. The unwillingness to have children in his past life led my patient to a tragically premature death. Now another form of punishment, even more severe, reached him in this life. A blood disorder, impervious to medical remedies, would cause the termination of his lineage if healing measures were not taken. For me, to meet someone to whom I was married in one of my past lives was a shock. But, due to my past family's position in the 1780s, I was pushed to marry this handsome, but older, German officer from the same class. He had illegitimate children, and chose not to have any children with me. He was not a family man, and continued to have affairs even after we had married. When he was killed in one of the numerous wars, I felt relief.

The connection between diseases without a cure and karmic derivations was well documented in one of my patients. The child, Laura, who was almost never sick, developed leukemia. What was the reason for this punishment of her and her parents? The analysis of her past life showed that she had lived dissolutely in the form of a man. As a robber and a bandit, Laura had caused the demise of many innocent souls, for which she – a quite guileless child – now was to suffer.

How many reincarnations or healing sessions are required to re-establish the energy fields of this girl? These energy structures, together with the fields of her parents and close family, create that mystical Karma. There is a chance of allaying it by adjusting the inner spiritual ties of the child with the Higher Power. I am speaking of that same Quasiworld where there are particular laws to which we submit daily without our knowledge, whether we want to or not, and which guides us without our realization.

After compiling material and responses from meetings with my clients, I formed the impression that the karmic cycle, never stops. It is eternal. We are eternally ordained to meet the same relatives and friends from life to life, and that cannot be avoided. We are changing only the trappings, the costumes and roles in that gigantic cosmic play performed under the guidance of an invisible director. The ruler of the Universe controls the quality of our performance through reward or reinforcement, through diverse methods if the predestined role is negligently performed. I cannot name the number of people with whom I met and whom I helped, for I haven't counted them. I know one thing: that in the majority of cases, the ones who ask for help have already received it from me in a past life. I cannot convey with words the energy fluxes that arise when meeting such people! Sometimes even mentioning their names, I feel indescribable sensations which tell me of the need to see them.

And what can I do with the facts that are impossible to dismiss? My cases seem to reflect the unending, accompanying action of invisible beings or quasi-forces who, during the course of treatment, don't leave their patients for the duration of the therapy, despite the distances and circumstances separating them. My patients have told me about many experiences that make it difficult to distinguish reality from fantasy, so I just have to trust them. Sometimes I wonder if all of this is just imagination! You can talk about fantasy when it happens once, but if it happens again and again, then it is a hidden pattern of natural law waiting to be revealed.

I cannot remember exactly when I learned about the continued action of quasi-forces after a session. From this point of view, it is interesting to relate the actions of "invisible friends" in the case of Anne. After reaching a turning point in her treatment, Anne told me about her experiences and sensations. While doing needlepoint at home after one session, she analyzed her emotions and her relationship with me. Out of nowhere, a selfish thought came into her mind: "Why should I pay Rachel for her work, which does not even deal with the material dimension and does not have value?" The struggle between dark and light spiritual forces continued until the light part of Anne's soul realized that I actually fulfill the role of the doctor, and the labor of the physician should be remunerated. So what difference does it make who gets paid? The doctor with the diploma or the doctor with the gift? The final result differs only in method.

As soon as her wondering soul accepted this decision about the importance of rewarding the healer's work, she felt the beneficial action of quasi-specialists, my assistants. Their delicate manipulations were unfolding within Anne and bringing her relief from session to session.

At the same time that she experienced agitated indecision, Anne received an explanation for some of her more bothersome questions. In her narration, the concept sounds like this: "To consider breaking the agreement about financial compensation for any previously negotiated healing work is a test by the quasi-forces, forcing a decision as to which is more important for you: the material world or your spiritual welfare, literally choosing between life and death. This is the only decision that everyone must make in one of the stages of life. The examination of spiritual maturity never passes us by, and everyone must go through it sooner or later."

We are all, by one way or another, connected with each other, and this is a generally recognized fact. Sometimes I cannot explain the unusual unfolding relationships at the spiritual level between me and my previous and current patients, but they contribute to the richness of our relationships, with their worlds of feelings mixed with memories of past lives, and delicate associations and precarious balance.

Occasionally I participate in the unfinished conflicts with invisible forces, and then I am left to fight with "appearing ghosts" in the true sense of the word. I never thought that this could happen. I have just completed another course of treatment with Anne, whose conversations were intellectually stimulating. During these talks, she has always received answers to her questions, but what is most interesting is that she posed them to me in an especially thought-provoking way, which I had to contemplate before replying.

During the weeks before starting the next stage of therapy sessions with Anne, I had felt, during the nights, that someone was not only trying to stop me from working with her but also was crushing me physically. Those unforgettable nights cannot be erased from my memory, especially one! I awakened after half an hour with an unclear sensation that it wasn't a time for sleeping, but to be on guard. I spent all night anxiously waiting for approaching disaster. I had an impression that my quasi-friends kept me ready for action. During one of my intermittent slumbers, I felt what seemed like some ghastly snake-like creatures began their activity in my liver. Thus, I realized what danger my invisible friends were trying to save me from. Unconsciously, our subconscious sends messages to alert and prepare us for action.

During sleep, the circumstances may change. Although the subconscious remain active, our physical body is relaxed and does not react to danger signals. Without fully awakening, I started to duel a pack of creatures, starting with the largest and finishing with the offspring. Gaining a victory, I returned to sleep for some time. The dream that came to me that night affirmed my victory over the forces of darkness.

Intuitively, I knew all of this was somehow connected with Anne, but I had never perceived my patients in any other way than as sick people who need my assistance. The following conversation with her confirmed my fears about the presence of some negative forces, affecting her destiny. During these nights, Anne had a similar spiritual experience. Despite the distance separating us, our physical activities during the following days were identical, as though we were twins.

The main idea in combating negative energies is not to stop halfway but to persist, which not everyone realizes. I thank my quasi-friends all the time for their support, knowing that there is much I have to accomplish in this world where positive and negative energies continuously battle.

During my long conversations with patients and friends and through my affiliation with the Quasiworld, I came to the conclusion that people can be separated into groups, according to their physic perception of the Quasiworld. You may choose which type relates to you:

- Perceiving the Quasiworld as an existing reality from the time of birth.
- Receiving the Quasiworld as a result of tragic life situations or trauma.
- Gaining access to the Quasiworld through healers or spiritual practices.
- Acknowledging the physical awareness of the Quasiworld without being able to see, hear, smell, taste or touch it.
- Believing in the existence of the Quasiworld, but not sensing it.
- Denying the existence of the Quasiworld, since it is still not acknowledged by conventional science.

Quasiworld is that unassailable element of the supernatural, existing since the ages of oblivion and unaffected by time, which has an unrecognized sphere of influence and direction to which humanity aspires to reach from day to day.

Every historical era gives birth to individuals who bear new ideas and theories for their times. These theories shape the consciousness of the next generation. People seldom realize that humanity's journey to knowledge aspires to one goal: to know oneself and one's soul, and that part of the Universe that connects us with it. The unity of spiritual and physical health of a human being can be attained through this search.

Who will become the next Einstein by developing a theory and researching the boundless Quasiworld, influencing the minds of the next generations, each in cosmic turn ...?

Chapter V

YOUR HEALTH
–
CHANCE OR
CHOICE?

Experience is never limited and it is never complete; it is an immense sensibility, a kind of huge spiderweb of the finest silken threads suspended in the chamber of consciousness and catching every airborne particle in its tissue.

–Henry James

The Job of Time

*I*t is the time to do the job,

The job of time and time of life
There is a door, a sacred door
The door of things that we don't know
The things that must not be forgotten
The place of peace that will come soon

It is time to do the job
The job of time, the time of life
The sooner we will find that time
That time that we are looking for
The hunt is on for the things we want
The goal of life that must be found

It is the time to do the job
The job of time, the time of life
The life is just the thing we need
The time that we must conquer now
The bridge of time that's standing strong
The bridge of time that could be broken
The bridge of life will try to save
That is the road of an eternity.

N. Madorsky

Having had a busy healing practice, having read a large volume of literature, and encountering various modes of treatment, I have come to the conclusion that in order to cure a living organism, there are no identical methods, just as there are no identical people. Just as we are not intended to repeat the creations of Rembrandt, so the work of the healer and the process of the patient's recovery are singular in their actions. Each has his own way of receiving the necessary information useful in the treatment of various diseases. The healer and the patient finally reach the result planned by both of them during sessions. Healers treat by herbs, diet, water, words, look, the transmission of thought across distance, crystals, or touch. The origin of the same problem in different people is unique. However, there is one thing that unites all healers: the heartfelt desire to help those who are suffering.

At the first symptoms of disease, a patient generally seeks consultation. The patient thinks that his mission has been completed, not suspecting that this is only a prelude to a personal battle. The physician who examines patients cannot take responsibility for their health. He only fulfills a technical role: diagnosing and prescribing medicine, which, at best, won't harm the patient. At times when medical therapists are unable to rid the patient of the disease, which actually happens in the majority of cancer cases, the dismayed patient turns to the surgeon. So what is really happening? When we enter the doctor's office, we are ready to relinquish our responsibility for the state of our health to him or her, often committing a fatal error. The healer determines the direction of the attack and rejuvenates the patient's defense mechanisms. Only our personal desire to be healthy gives additional strength. Everybody can find the information he or she is looking for. The main idea is to rouse the motivation to search for truth and self-knowledge to take a chance to make a choice.

When does the process of healing begin? It is when there is an unalterable wish to change something in oneself. Although sometimes the reason is unknown, the soul of the afflicted seeks help, knocks in the heart, insistently asking for attention from consciousness. At the moment the person in pain becomes aware of the necessity to search for help, everything starts to take on a lighter shade and change for the better. This is what happened to a young woman who came to visit me.

Sara P. was searching for the answers to her problems for quite some time, believing that their solution depended on her. She had attended numerous sessions with another healer who also treated her husband. However, the situation did not improve. To the contrary, it became more complicated. My examination traced many of Sara's ailments to her gastrointestinal tract, which was affected not only by the stressful relationship with her spouse, but also, as was clear from a distance diagnosis of him, the presence of cancer in his body. Her soul had realized the imminent danger threatening the family.

After the session, I decided to answer her questions concerning her husband. I advised her to treat him like a child, and, during his sickness, forgive all his fancies, but not forget the necessity of treating the disorder. How the danger will be perceived by her spouse and what actions he will take is not yet known, but the treatment has begun. Possibly, by the time this book is published, I shall add something about the fate of this young man.

When someone calls me asking for an emergency visit and I do not feel there is need for urgency, I usually schedule the appointments in a couple of weeks or months. It is quite feasible for the caller to solve the problem himself during this period.

Sometimes the sudden desire to fight for his own health will overtake him without pressure from the family, which does not wish to remain indifferent. In some difficult situations, I conduct a preliminary distance determination before the visit of the potential patient.

An interesting case occurred involving an iridology doctor and me. Iridology is the science of investigating connections between the change of hues in the iris and the condition of the body's organs. At my request, we decided to conduct a clean experiment, to verify the credibility of both his and my methods of diagnosis. At our meeting, I brought separate sealed envelopes with the results of my distance testing of him and his wife. Nobody knows our past and possible present ailments better than ourselves, but who is granted knowledge of the problems awaiting us?

A distance diagnosis consists of mentally scanning all physiological systems and organs with simultaneous information retrieval from the world data bank. Everyone is given a specified chamber in the cosmic computer's universal memory, where all the information about us is continuously transmitted and kept. The CosComp is a computer unyielding to viruses which are capable of erasing the information in one instant. Remember this always! The megacomputer of the Universe works without delay. Imagine that you are the operator of the control and tracking station of the life support of the human body and your duty is to monitor the functions of the station. In case of accidental failure of the automatic system of control and regulation, you take responsibility for the fate of the human being and the people surrounding him. What is necessary is the will, and each of us can master the technique of requesting and managing this immediate means of psychic first aid.

We met in a properly equipped physician's office. First my husband and I were examined. Then I scanned the doctor and his wife with my palms. Since I had knowledge of iridology and its results, the doctor was somewhat shocked by the similarity of the results together with the prognostication of "my" method. The method of iridology is valuable in establishing past diseases as well as the development of new ones, but the method of accessing the universal computer cannot be compared to anything in order to evaluate it.

Opening the envelopes after testing, we compared the results – they matched almost exactly. The only difference was that, using the cosmic diagnosis, I was not interested in the diseases that have passed and do not influence the present time. My readings concentrated upon those unfolding now or expected in the near future.

The iris reading allows diagnosis of changes in the body which could be measured by other official medical methods if utilized correctly. I am registering deviations which haven't yet manifested themselves on the physical level, but which are clearly marked, or appear, according to karma, on the external energy field (aura).

There was no limit to the astonishment of the doctor and his wife. But there was only one problem: I wasn't supposed to tell them about all their diseases. On a one-to-one basis, I have revealed to each of them the specific illnesses which are detectable in advance, and named the ones that already exist. These are their personal secrets, which in time must be disclosed to each other, as they cannot be fought alone because of the imperative moral support in the struggle with health problems. Receiving a positive confirmation from one of them about a history of cancer in the family, I warned them to take preventive measures.

This was such an interesting experiment! As it turned out, both methods work and can be used without a doubt, as the practice has already completed its trials for many centuries.

I have also compared my diagnostic methods with others. The conclusion: it does not matter how the diagnosis is determined, because the source of information is one – the Cosmos. However I advise you as the reader to ask for opinions from different sources, as this is more reliable. I prefer a distance method to the local one. In the local technique, by use of the palms, overlap between energy vibrations is sometimes possible. At times, however, the perception of ultra-weak vibrations of barely discernible illness gives a slightly gloomier picture. It is the same as looking at the paintings of the Impressionists. Standing near, you distinguish only the dots, but at a distance you embrace with a glance an indescribable beauty. At the optimal viewpoint, the full picture of the physical condition of the examined organism is clearly and objectively visible.

In conversing with a potential patient, we establish a psychological contact and prepare ourselves to begin the course of treatment. I prefer the patient to be standing, so the whole body surface can be examined, but lying down is also satisfactory. Due to my innate left-handedness, I have equally developed both hands. Therefore, I unconsciously examine with both hands. They move parallel to each other along the body, having a chance to simultaneously register and compare the signals received from the epicenter of emission.

For example, aberrations in heart function are perceived more easily from the back. Independent of my personal desire, the process of treatment starts when I extend my hand for diagnosis or for demonstration of the essence of bioenergetic impact on the human body. When a reaction to my energy proceeds in the form of a feeling of warmth, cold, light breeze, pressure or pricking, and in some cases, the appearance of shivering, etc., the treatment occurs faster because the patient does not resist psychologically.

It is possible that such responses arise because we encountered each other in one of our previous lives. At the time of contact between our energy fields, the memory of the past possibly reminds us about past meetings, more likely, about familiar experience, telling you that everything will be well if you trust your subconscious.

I scan from top to bottom with simultaneous regional magnification, i.e., with horizontal movements and mental retrieval of the specificity of the physiological aberration in the organ or system at a distance of 10-15 cm or 4 to 6 inches from the body surface. My fingers or palms track signals of different quality and intensity. These could be the signals of a disease-carrying nature, up to the energy stroke, or in the shape of a dense screen, not admitting a stranger. Chronic conditions manifest themselves by weaker signals. The location of a cold field testifies to the presence of a tumor; but the unparalleled, unpleasant sensation like touching dry ice alerts and prepares me for cancer.

Each healer approaches the process of examination with his own well-tried methods. Each way is good in determining a correct diagnosis. I try to diagnose and give my therapy sessions in a room with a faucet and sink. I wash my hands with water if I find a serious signal while scanning the patient and, as a rule, at the completion of the session.

Place your hands for a short time near the flame of a candle or other torchlight. It is often sufficient to raise the energy potential of one's body to quite a high level. The presence of a burning flame during my work on patients is one of the definite attributes of my practice. The flame of a candle or of other natural source of fire is believed to cleanse out the space, destroying many harmful energy formations emerging as a result of "undesirable" thoughts or human actions. Fire is the only natural source of positive energy. In all cultures, it performs its part in purification, healing and unifying of the substance. For your own use, light the number of candles with which you feel comfortable.

A British museum displays an ancient Egyptian parchment, dated 1550 B.C., which contains a schematic representation of energy centers and meridians of the human body. It might be noted that some of its parts – the face, nose, ears, eyes, and feet – contain regions related to internal organs. Acupuncture was widely known in the countries of the South Pacific and in the Arabic east. The famous philosopher and physician Avicenna (980-1037 AD), investigating the problems of acupuncture in his work, developed the concept of meridians – energy channels.

Chakras

I finish the local and distance scanning by checking the function of energy centers (chakras), through which the exchange of energy with the Cosmos occurs. I will attempt to describe in some detail the seven main centers located on the vertical axis of the human body, since not everyone has had the chance to hear or read about them (Fig. 5-1). More complete information about the major, as well as the additional chakras, located not only on the palms and feet but also in the areas of joints, etc., is available in books on the topic.

Different cultures name the energy centers differently, but the name "chakra" is widespread. In Sanskrit it means "wheel of light." These seven chakras reflect our essence, what we feel, how we think, and how we change. The chakras are the energy gates of the body, through which the energy reaches us, and discharges from us. The exchange of energy must be balanced; otherwise, discrepancies occur in the body. Although most sources pinpoint only seven major chakras, in reality, there are more than 360 of them distributed throughout the human body.

Each main chakra is connected to one of the major nerve plexuses regulating various functions of the internal organs and one of the major endocrine glands. Without going into much detail about the nervous plexuses and endocrine glands, I'd like to give you a short description of their relationship with the main chakras.

• The first, or base chakra is located in the area of the sacral plexus. This governs the internal, mostly vascular plexuses of cavernous bodies and the lower portion of the rectum. This area also includes the reproductive glands. This chakra is responsible for the reproductive functions and for the will to live (Fig. 5-1a).

• The second chakra is located a bit lower than the navel at the position of the lumbar plexus regulating the vegetative reflexes of the urinary-sexual systems and legs. That is also where the adrenal glands are located (Fig. 5-1b).

• The third chakra is located at the level of the solar plexus. It is a large accumulation of nerve fibers located in front of the abdominal aorta. It fills the space formed by the three most important arteries of the abdominal cavity, the liver, spleen, and stomach arteries, which branch off from the abdominal aorta. This is the area of the pancreas. The activity of the whole body, and also the brain, depends on the function of this chakra (Fig. 5-1c).

• The fourth, or the cardiac, chakra is placed in the center of the cardiac aortal plexus. It regulates blood circulation of the body, with the exception of circulation in the brain. The thymus gland joins the area of this plexus, the role of which is crucial in the immune defense of the body (Fig. 5-1d).

•   The fifth chakra, the chakra of the larynx, is situated in the area of the plexus of the carotid arteries, located on the level of the larynx, and is involved in the regulation of the blood circulation in the brain. At the base of the skull there is also a poorly differentiated plexus carrying vegetative innervation. It is mainly composed of the vagus and trifacial nerves. In the area of the larynx, there are also the thyroid and parathyroid glands. This chakra is the connecting link between physical and spiritual initiatives of the person (Fig. 5-1e).

•   The sixth chakra, called the Third Eye, is located on the bridge of the nose, between the brows. It corresponds to ganglia of the tenth and fifth pair of cranial nerves. It is the means of abstraction from concrete forms. Behind this chakra, the pituitary, pineal glands, and hypothalamus are positioned (Fig. 5-1f).

•   The seventh chakra corresponds to the brain and has a spiritual aspect. It is responsible for the spiritual connections with Universe (Fig. 5-1g).

When all chakras rotate with the normal speed clockwise and have a certain diameter, the body can indeed be in excellent health. When one or more chakras change their characteristics, it indicates the onset of serious deviations in the organism or the beginning of aging.

Chakras are tuned to specific cosmic energy vibration frequencies; however, their functions do not reach complete development and maturity until the age of 30. After they have matured, they are ready to demonstrate the highest degrees of proficiency. Therefore, I remind you again, that the healers who would like to pursue occultist practice can only engage in this activity upon reaching the age of 30.

During the chakra's rotation, its specific electromagnetic field emerges. By combining with the fields created by other centers, it creates a common field around the body which we call a bioenergetic field, or aura. Due to this interconnection, if the individual has some aberration in his body or is sick, it makes no real difference which chakra the healer is focused on, for the problem will be solved. During a continual treatment of one of the chakras, the rest simultaneously restore their functions. By means of chakras, the bioenergetic field maintains an extensively

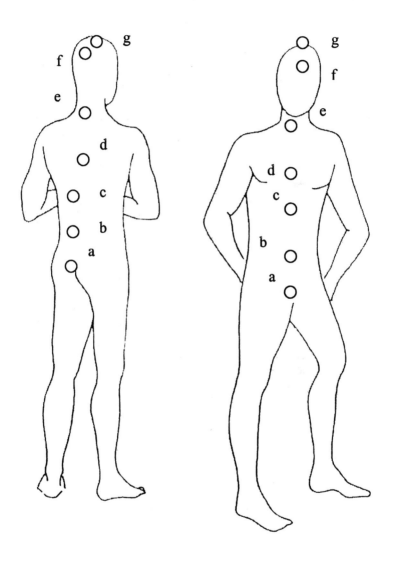

Fig. 5-1

organized connection with the whole system of energy channels, otherwise known as meridians, to which we will return later.

I finish my physical energetic examination with an investigation of the energy centers, confirming my suspicions regarding strong energy transformations in the body. For this purpose I use a crystal quartz pendulum. When this is not available, one can use any suitable object, from a ring to a button, suspended on a thread. The length of the thread is usually 20-25 cm, or 8 to 10 inches. When the pendulum is suspended over a chakra, counterclockwise movement usually signals an energy block.

Following the assessment, the data is analyzed and compared with the information presented by the patient in an interview. Patients frequently attempt to conceal unpleasant facts, which I generally do not challenge. Sooner or later, they will be uncovered anyway.

When a serious condition like cancer is present, the conversation is directed to family history, with a focus on genetics. At such moments, the healer is one-on-one with his conscience and personal responsibility, placed on him at the time of the decision to offer the diagnosis. It is the most tormenting step: to tell or not to tell. If one is instructed to tell, then what will be the reaction of the patient when official medical technology is still unable to determine a correct prognosis in the initial stage of the disease found in the energy field, but not yet in the body? In any case, I insist on a visit to the doctor for laboratory testing. I also sometimes advise the patient to elaborate on his suffering so that the doctor will be able to sympathize and prescribe more detailed examination.

In the energy treatment, we must attempt to connect the manifestation of the given disease with the patient's family karma, and with the fate of previous generations. We must never overlook the role of previous incarnations to which we are tied. Usually in such cases, the discussion is prolonged, and sometimes afterwards the patient does not return until months or years later, when he rushes in with a plea for assistance. Eventually the choice is made for the sake of the living and the continuation of the family line.

From this time on, the process of recovery is initiated: slow and drawn out in one case, and quite rapid in another.

Breathing Exercises

Before the beginning of each session, I always recommend that my patients do breathing gymnastics throughout the therapy. This practice allows them to divert their attention from negative thoughts with simultaneous visualization of light currents. Begin with a simple exercise; on the count of 3, each count being about one second long. Inhale, hold the breath for 3 counts, then exhale during 3 counts, and before the next inhalation hold still for 3 counts. Repeat each exercise during the whole session, 3-3-3-3. With time, when you learn to do it during the day for several minutes, I recommend increasing the intervals to 4-4-4-4, reaching a maximum of 8-10-8-10. It is most important to hold your breath before exhaling. In this moment, the body is absorbing the maximum amount of cosmic energy taken during the inhalation. I sometimes try to exhale inside myself, imagining how this air energy pours into my cells, filling them with vital energy.

There is more than enough literature available about the methods of breathing, and you can choose one which suits you best. Indian yoga has a well developed system of breathing exercises which I recommend. It is generally known that oxygen enters the brain during inhalation through the nose. I simply adore the following old yoga breathing exercise. Plug your right nostril with your thumb, and press the index finger on the third eye, making a deep, slow inhalation (3-8 seconds). Hold your breath for 3 to 8 seconds. Then, freeing the right nostril, close up the left nostril with the middle finger, but leave the index finger in its original position while exhaling for 3 to 8 seconds. Hold the finger position for 3 to 8 seconds, inhale again with the right nostril, make a similar pause for 3 to 8 seconds, then close up the right nostril with the thumb, and exhale on the left side. This exercise uses both solar and lunar energy and stimulates the development of the third eye. Start with four cycles two times a day and work up to eight. In due time you will feel infused with a surge of spiritual energy.

During inhalation, I recommend that my patients imagine a flowing light entering their bodies, and during exhalation, they should imagine themselves under a plummeting waterfall, where the currents of water rid them of all wastes and instill in them an indefinable feeling of energy saturation.

I also ask my patients to play out in their imagination battles in which they conquer the cancer cells. Cancer cells are as prone to psychological impact as normal cells. They react to messages sent by the brain, and one can attain amazing results by acting on them in a particular fashion. Any mental scenario that leads to victory for the attacker-patient produces positive results, as has been confirmed. This resembles the psychological mindset of the athlete before competition, when he is committed to victory at any price. You cannot deny a winner!

When working with tumors and metastasis, I do not advise the healer to direct the stream of energy to the sites of illness during initial sessions; wait until after the immune and endocrine systems are partially restored. I often have to deal with serious diseases and, as a result of considerable experience, I have found an interesting principle. The more serious the state of the patient is, the more time his moral and psychological preparation takes before we can proceed with the process of recovery. At the same time, the length of the session is inversely proportional to the time of preparation and the physical health of the patient. The more the patient is weakened, the shorter the therapy session. One is forced to start with a few minutes, preferably on a daily basis, extending it to 15-20 minutes, with subsequent transition into sessions 3-times-a-week, then to 2-times-a-week, gradually switching to once a week. The process of decreasing the number of sessions happens slowly, giving the body a chance to get used to its forgotten responsibilities while the immune system is regaining charge of the situation.

During a session, I offer some people a chair; others have to remain standing, and still others I ask to lie down on the massage table. Everything depends upon the seriousness of the problem. When it is not necessary to target the whole body, I hold my palms over the organ of interest at a distance of 5-10 cm or 2 to 4 inches or position my palms around it. I call a parallel position of the palms "the sandwich" – the most effective in my practice. I keep my healing hands over part of a patient's body until the perceived signal is weakened. Sometimes I place them over the surface of the body. I never do sessions with bare parts of the patient's body exposed, to avoid both hygiene concerns as well as emotional discomfort for the patient and me. I ask patients to come for treatment in clothes made from natural fibers. Best of all are clothes made from cotton. Removing various adornments, watches, or belts simplifies the flow of therapy.

During sessions, I sometimes use a method of treatment through breath. I flow cold or hot air through my mouth over a certain body area. The air, filled with my bioenergy, when entering the affected organs, enhances the healing effect. Interesting sensations are produced in the patients during this process, ranging from the feeling of piercing cold or heat to rising pressure on the sick organ.

All parents remember that indescribable feeling of bliss which permeated them and the absolute delight of the baby when they blow air into the child's navel. How many happy emotions were aroused in both! In this moment, the parents are unconsciously feeding their children with the indispensable energy for growth, which babies need so much at the first stage of their life. Do it more often, and you will see how contact with your baby improves. These ties will never disappear, and will subconsciously be preserved through life.

In complicated situations, my session consists of three or four parts. There is no particular sequence to this, as everything proceeds intuitively and depends on many circumstances, including weather. At the beginning of the session in most cases, I ask for permission from the Higher Forces, emphasizing that the patient carries his own personal responsibility for the process of recovery. Or I simply pray to God with my own prayer.

Mentally, I ask the quasi-assistants to take part in treatment of the patient. The particular specialists necessary for the given circumstances usually always arrive. Sometimes there is only one working, but usually several take turns during brief periods of time and their manipulations and hand motions differ. There is a variety of such movements, and all of them are interesting and captivating. I never found it possible to simply repeat them for the sake of pleasure.

There were only a few cases in my practice when the quasi-forces refused to work through me with the patient. Those patients had a different outlook for the world than the quasi-assistants. The quasi-assistants do not accept lies, so these patients and I went our different ways.

I am convinced that if you have an enormous desire to help yourself and others, unparalleled quasi-colleagues will come to answer your call. Be diligent in your attempts to work with quasi-forces, and they will support people with pure spiritual thoughts. They will not only give assistance to others around you, but they will also come to you personally. Believe that! Many times they have simply saved me from pains caused by long, exhilarating work. They have even foiled attempts of certain occult specialists to act upon my energy field just out of their curiosity trying to compare my abilities with theirs!

My experience has shown that the use of my quasi-colleagues' expertise hastens the correction of energy fields surrounding any living or nonliving matter and cleanses everything extraneous and harmful. The sensations perceived by the human body at these times include fluctuations in the movement of air, internal cold, light phenomena, weightlessness, and unclear displacements inside the body. In such cases the patients perceive both physical and emotional relaxation, which allows them to consider the situation more sensibly and quietly, without panic. The restoration of external, invisible "tissues" leads to revival of the normal function in physiological systems and affected organs. I'd like to remind you that I am no different from my patient while working with quasi-forces. I merely am an intermediary in transmitting energy and the knowledge of nature and become a common tool in the hands of the Higher Forces of Nature.

Another thing I do is to run the tips of my fingers across the spinal cord as though along a piano keyboard, relieving the energy blocks generated in separate vertebrae. This area is one of the central mechanisms of energy exchange in the body and its function in vigorous activity is extremely important. The information transmitted from the brain to internal organs descends along the spinal column, which is one of the largest accumulators of subtle energy, and furthers on through spinal nerves supplying the outlying areas of the organism. After the spinal cord, I usually proceed to relieve energy blocks in the network of energy channels located in the physical body of the patient, increasing circulation of the energy currents. I will try to give a brief introduction to my understanding of the energy channels and meridians.

Meridians

According to Eastern medicine, the human body is an inseparable part of the Universe. Its life activity is constantly affected by the influence of transforming forces of the environment, directed by the same powers and laws that act upon the Universe. In order to function normally, the human being receives a certain amount of energy from the mother at birth and, during all his life, from the macrocosm. This energy is present in both the microcosm human being and also in the macrocosm, which is the world around us. Thus, energy exists both outside and inside the body.

The functioning of the organs is supported by the consistent circulation of two components of internal energy constantly flowing through the body along the closed system of energy channels or meridians. Disruption in the work of the meridians summons disease, manifested by the unequal distribution of energy in body organs, while the cessation of its movement leads to death. Therefore, treatment must be applied to the restoration of normal energy circulation in the channels.

The meridians have been measured, and an updated chart of their positions was compiled with the help of scientific methods: electric, thermographic, and radioactive. With practice, one can perceive them with the fingertips. There is a certain number of acupuncture points along the meridians. These points connect the positive and negative meridians with the functional organs and muscles. The twelve classical meridians are used for diagnostic and curative purposes. Currently, there are about 800 known points (there are another 147 acupuncture points and 8 new meridians, in addition to 14 found on the chart). Acupuncturists use about 365 points in daily practice.

The meridians listed below are named according to crucial organs and systems with which they are possibly connected, but the energy blocks in them do not indicate the presence of physical changes in the organs. A traditional Chinese physician can determine the imbalance in a certain channel by feeling the pulse. The following are the main meridians:

• The pericardium meridian or the meridian of the cardiovascular and sexual sphere starts from the tip of a middle finger, ascends up along the hand and stops at the chest, just a little bit away from the nipple (Fig. 5-2a). The influence of the pericardium meridian stimulates the blood circulation and metabolism, significantly affecting psychological disorders.

• The meridian of the liver begins at the outer edge of the nail root of the big toe, then extends along the inner surface of the leg, passes to the anterior surface of the torso, and stops in the area under the chest in the 6th intercostal space (Fig. 5-2b). The meridian of the liver is involved in cases of diseases of the sexual organs and functional problems of the excretory system. In a number of skin diseases, this meridian is coordinated with the meridian of the lungs.

• The meridian of the three parts of the torso, or the triple warmer, proceeds from the nail root of the ring finger, ascends along the hand, along the back side of the shoulder, along the neck, encircles around the earlobe, and stops at the exterior end of the brow (Fig. 5-3a). This is the meridian of the endocrine system. The specificity of location of the three-part meridian of the torso makes it possible to act upon the diseases of the head, problems in the chest and abdominal areas, and also in the urinary-sexual system.

• The meridian of the gallbladder starts near the exterior edge of the eye, reaches the earlobe, encircles it, follows the sideline of the head, descends through the neck into the area over the shoulder blades, passes along the side surface of the sternum and farther down along the side surface of the leg. It ends near the nail root of the fourth toe (Fig. 5-3b). This meridian is associated with various aches, as well as diseases of the gallbladder and the branching ducts.

• The lung meridian travels from the second rib to the shoulder and descends along the hand to the nail root of the thumb (Fig. 5-4a). The lung meridian is treated for diseases of the breathing organs and bronchial asthma. It is also targeted during a number of skin diseases.

• The meridian of the spleen ascends from the nail root of the big toe up along the inner surface of the leg, passes along the frontal abdominal wall reaching the second intercostal space, then down to the side, ceasing at the 7th intercostal space (Fig. 5-4b). Action over the spleen meridian normalizes the function of the digestive channel, liver, pancreas, lungs, and spleen.

• The meridian of the kidney begins from the middle of the sole of the foot, ascends along the inner surface of the leg, along the anterior abdominal wall, and stops near the lower edge of the clavicle (Fig. 5-5a). The kidney meridian affects stagnant phenomena in the chest cavity during bronchial asthma and stenocardia, regulates the urinary-sexual and digestive systems, and also influences the personality.

• The meridian of the small intestine originates at the tip of the pinkie, ascends along the hand and the back surface of the shoulder, proceeds along the side surface of the neck, and separates into two branches: one stretching along the cheek to the earlobe, and another into the interior angle of the eye (Fig. 5-5b). The meridian of the small intestine is the target during the treatment of nervous, rheumatic, and arthritic illnesses.

• The meridian of the urinary bladder begins near the interior angle of the eye, ascends to the area of the forehead, follows the top of the head, diverges into two branches on the back surface of the neck, which, in turn, pass along the back and the back surface of the thigh, converging in the pit behind the knee and terminating at the tip of the little toe (Fig. 5-6a). This meridian is treated during pain spasms, aches, and also in the case of chronic skin disorders.

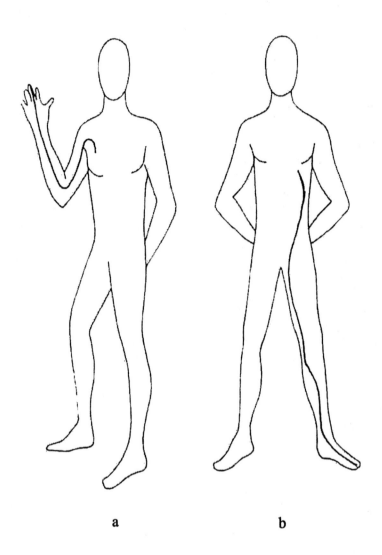

a   b

Fig. 5-2

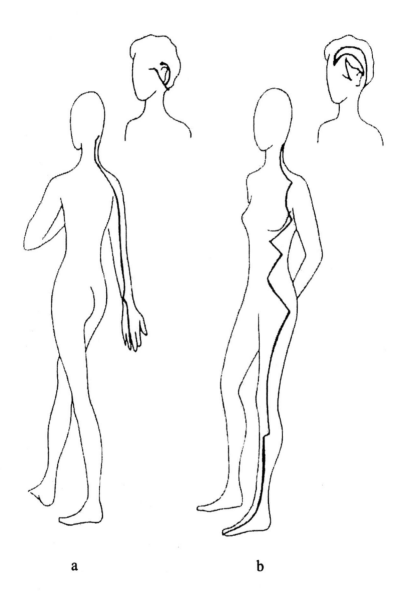

a   b

Fig. 5-3

• The meridian of the large intestine starts at the tip of the index finger, runs up along the hand, neck, and face, and stops in the upper portion of the nasolabial furrow (Fig. 5-6b). The meridian of the large intestine is mainly treated in diseases of the stomach, large intestine, lungs, mucous membranes and skin. It is also recommended for aching syndromes of the torso.

• The meridian of the stomach springs from the middle of the lower edge of the eye, passes along the cheek, descends through the frontal surface of the torso and leg, and goes along the foot until it reaches the nail root of the second toe (Fig. 5-7a). The stomach meridian affects diseases of the gastrointestinal tract, nervous system, the larynx, teeth and fever.

• The heart meridian originates in the heart, follows the upper frontal corner of the armpit, descends along the hand to the palm towards the nail root of the pinkie (Fig. 5-7b). The meridian of the heart is mainly related to the functional state of the heart and circulation, and is correspondingly used in treating various emotional and stress-related illnesses or depression.

• The posterior medial meridian begins in the lower pelvis and enters between the coccyx and anus, following the midline of the spinal column. It passes along the surface of the head and ends in the middle of the upper lip (Fig. 5-8a). The posterior and anterior medial meridians are used rarely, primarily for research purposes and for determining the functions of certain organs.

• The anterior medial meridian starts in the area situated between the external sexual organs and the anus, follows the abdominal, chest, and neck midline, and terminates in the center of the chin-lip fissure (Fig. 5-8b). This meridian is treated for diseases of the urinary tract, gastrointestinal tract, respiratory system, mouth cavity, and personality disorders.

I have noticed that the treatment of some organs proceeds more successfully at certain times of the day. I found support for this in the Chinese traditional healing school. Below is a biological schedule. However, it is practically impossible to synchronize the schedule of the patient's rhythm, my own, the biological hours of the sick organs, and, in addition, solar or lunar hours, which affect everyone without exception.

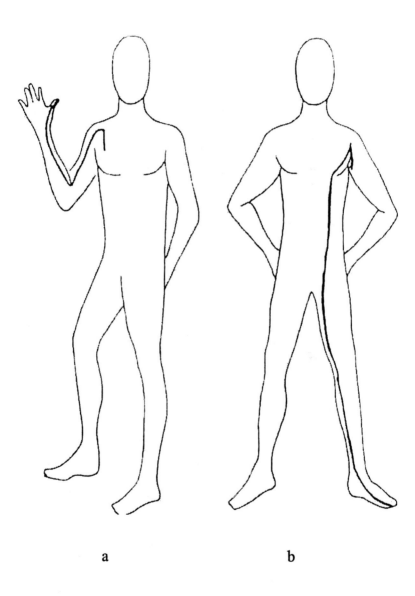

a   b

Fig. 5-4

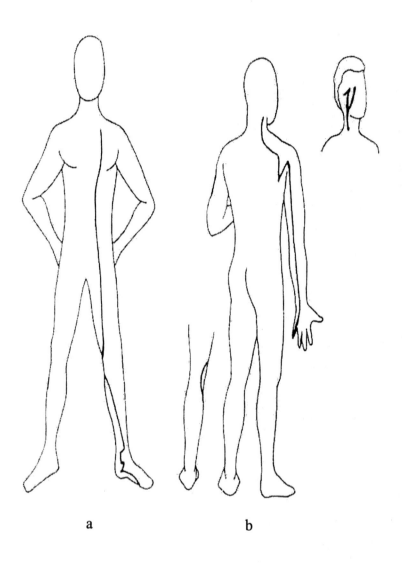

a   b

Fig. 5-5

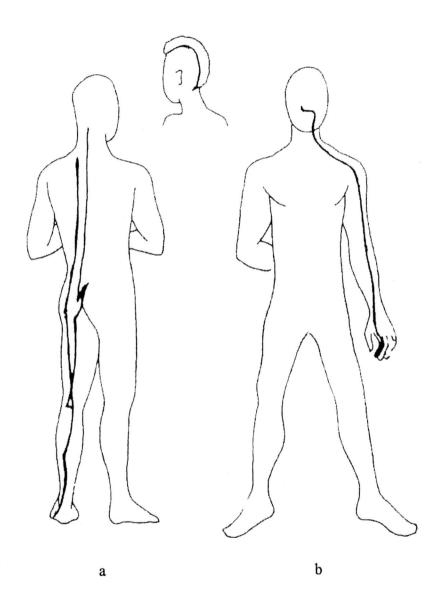

a

b

Fig. 5-6

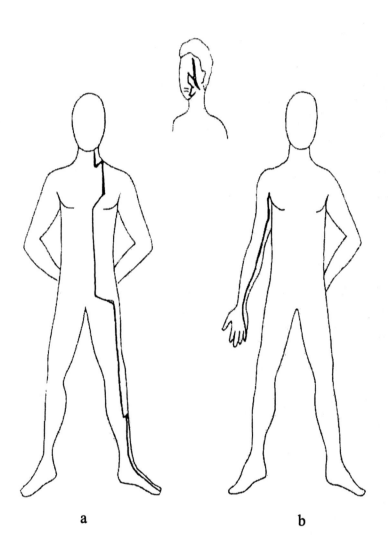

a   b

Fig. 6-7

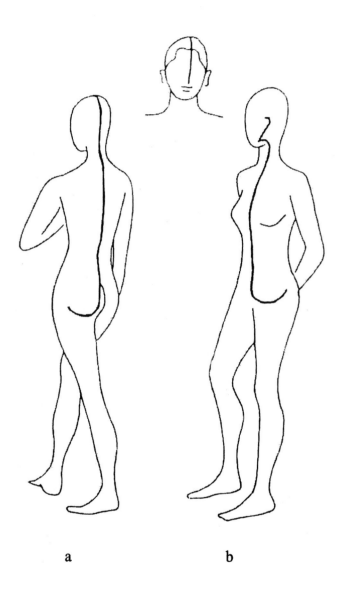

a   b

Fig. 6-8

The effect of the moon on particular days of treatment has the same importance as the weather. The lunar horoscope pinpoints the more favorable treatment days of the lunar month, which are counted from the New Moon. The best days for therapy are considered to be the 8th, 11th, 14th, 16th, 21st and 25th days, and the bad ones, the 3rd, 5th, 12th, 13th, and 29th.

To develop specific abilities of the psyche, the days that are especially favored are the 1st, 4th, 6th, and 14th, and the undesirable ones are the same as for treatment.

Biorhythmic periods

1am-3am	Liver	1pm-3pm	Small Intestine
3am-5am	Lungs	3pm-5pm	Bladder
5am-7am	Large intestine	5pm-7pm	Kidney
7am-9am	Stomach	7pm-9pm	Pericardium
9am-11am	Spleen	9pm-11pm	Triple warmer
11am-1pm	Heart	11pm-1am	Gallbladder

The above table of the twelve-hour periods of the day corresponds to the twelve zones of the Zodiac. According to the table, each classical meridian has a two-hour period during which the energy circulating in it reaches the maximal magnitude both in the associated organ and the meridian itself. When you feel a sense of constant discomfort recurring at the same time of day, take a look at the biorhythmic table. Be assured that you will find the answer to what organ is the source of your unpleasant sensations. For example, if, according to this table, you always had a bowel movement between 5am and 7am, then there would be no need for medications or enemas.

During healing sessions, often during the first consultation, I give a number of recommendations. The patient should acknowledge them and carry them out. My task is only to acquaint the patients with procedures that have been successful in my practice or the practice of other healers, or have been confirmed by current research.

Chapter VI

PRACTICING
WHAT
I PREACH

Prepare yourself that you must act alone.
The teacher may only point the way.
              −The Book of Golden Rules

Vision

We see our faces in the mirror the way we want to see

With eyes of deception we see our dream in life
To judge the people the way we feel is right for us
The making of decision depend on strength we have inside
Strength of our courage makes it happen
The getting the toys of our dream is the goal
Continue on to be deceiver of the others in our life of time
Other try to take us down and kill our time to be the future
Future we will make to have our vision of the life
Life of place and time to come and make it happen for us all.

N. Madorsky

Years ago, while I was waiting for a patient to come to my office, I cut my finger very deeply on my left hand. It was bleeding profusely and would not stop. It happened twenty minutes prior to the arrival of my patient so I had no time to go to the emergency room. Instead, I pictured myself as a little girl, sitting in a hidden place and talking with wounded parts of my body. This time I decided to call upon the wisdom of our ancients using incantations. From my collection of charms from around the world, I chose one with which I felt comfortable. Trying to keep damaged skin of the wounded area together, numerous times I repeated an incantation over my wound. It was miracle! Without needing stitches, the wound was healed and the bleeding stopped. I only covered that spot with a bandage as a protective measure. Many stories and tales are written about people who have the ability to stop bleeding, but this time it happened to me. I was relieved, but had no time to analyze this accident and healing; my patient was waiting. Later, I used these charms again. I speak with my body when it needs my help since we humans have the gift to talk with the body and the body will listen. Sometimes the right words come when we desperately need them.

To Stop a Blood Discharge

"I, the God's servant, (name), pass from doors to doors, from gates into gates, into a clear field, to the Eastern side. On the Eastern side there stands a cathedral of the Lord. Three girls are sitting in the Lord's Cathedral, the sisters by blood. They are sitting and sewing up horses with different silks. One has the horse of chestnut hue, no revel for the God's servant (name)! Another has the speckled horse, no drops will fall from God's servant, (name)! The other has the bay horse, no more blood for the God's servant, (name)!"

However, do not rely solely on charms to stop serious bleeding. Although it worked for me and for others, there are many factors to its power, including how connected you are to the Higher Forces. Although this is wisdom of our ancients, we live in a modern world and have to use its knowledge too. If you have serious injuries, go to the hospital! Don't delay!

I sometimes enjoy conversing with the afflicted organs during the session, sometimes in the manner of an instructor or a parent. I give them strict recommendations and orders, and implore them to change their behavior. You see, every cell in the body is capable of thinking, comprehending the information, and making a decision. It is very important for both the patient and the healer to find common ground with the body. Try to converse more often with those parts of the body which demand your heightened attention.

The spiritual qualities of the patient, together with his religious and psychological connections with the creator of the Universe, play a significant role in the efficiency and quantity of the sessions. Internal denial of the existence of the Higher Forces delays recovery. I mention all of this, not because being sick should force you to change your mindset, but only so you can acknowledge the presence of those forces which help us in the hard times of our lives. Those who live in large urban areas accept the necessity for contact with nature reluctantly. The loss of connections with natural cures have led to unnatural chemical methods of treatment and to the growth of diseases previously unheard of.

In special cases, such as cancer-related illnesses, I insist that patients pray with true repentance to God, the Creator of the Universe, with requests for forgiveness for all reckless deeds committed either by one's parents or ancestors. Why the law of Karma works in such an interesting way is not for us to judge. While reciting a prayer, it is imperative to feel a true repentance for what happened and cannot be changed, but for which we must pay through such terrible suffering. Pray for your loved ones in the same manner, but also ask for a blessing for their deliverance by the Higher Forces.

Forgiveness for Karmic Situations*

Oh, Lord, do not let us go against your will.
Lord, let us know the reasons for our disease.
Lord, let us find you in our search for the truth.
Lord, grant me deliverance from my sins and crimes
in the name of life.
Lord, give me your blessing in the name of my salvation.
Lord, give me your touch to my suffering soul.
Lord, I ask you to condescend to my sins, accumulated
through centuries.
Lord, I ask for forgiveness and forgetfulness for my past deeds.
Lord, I ask for the cure and recovery to my body, and in my soul,
the salvation from devilish designs.
Amen! Amen! Amen!

I wouldn't have included this advice in this book had it not been tried on my patients where I observed its result. During prayer, a spiritual cleansing occurs which no one can conduct except the one who prays. The advice given does not ask for any particular sacrifices. You have only to spend some time alone and then everything will change in your life!

Following my intuition regarding the treatment process, I come to the balancing of energy centers which in many countries of the world are called "chakras," from the Hindu word mentioned earlier. In situations that have become issues of control, one has to restore cosmic energy into each chakra or, sometimes, into selected ones. When the body is severely weakened, other methods of energy transmission should be used. All who have observed children have noticed how they enjoy spinning around in the middle of a room until they are exhausted. We, as adults, waltz with pleasure. I wouldn't have given this much thought, but for a case that evolved many years ago.

At a friend's house, I watched her son standing in the middle of the room and making circular movements without stopping. Five years passed before I visited them again. To my astonishment, I found the son grown to a young, stout fellow, 6'3" tall. Both his parents and grandparents were of short stature. It was amazing how one of his favorite pastimes, which upset the psychological equilibrium of the whole family, led to such an unexpected result.

Many years later, I decided to incorporate the lesson into my practice. Considering that all that is living evolves in a spiral, and all our energy chakras move clockwise in a normal state, I began this spinning exercise myself and recommend it to patients. I discovered that using this exercise succeeded in restoring the rotation of the energy centers. It is crucial to turn around only clockwise, starting with a few movements and increasing gradually to no more than 30, which is quite sufficient for the stimulation and nourishment of the chakras. Use this exercise as a component of your revitalizing exercises.

When working with meridians and chakras, I simultaneously conduct visual transmissions of energy to the endocrine, lymphatic, and cardiovascular systems. I also estimate the activity of all endocrine ducts. The process occurs smoothly. The main thing is not to rush. As the result of an intensified quasi-energy surge, an energy saturation of the organism occurs. This leads to a temporary and abrupt aggravation of the disease process and demands a special approach to healing. Since all this is ephemeral, it requires a significant mobilization of vital and psychic resources in coping with the healing crisis during the stages of recuperation.

The session is usually finished with a so-called quasi-operation or "psychic surgery." It occurs in the area where the affected organ is located. The sensations experienced by the patients are narrated in the chapter devoted to quasi-forces.

I place my hands on a certain spot of the body designated beforehand with the palms facing down. In some cases, the palms are placed together, but in others they make the shape of a "sandwich." The palms, positioned parallel to the body and to each other, become powerful emitters of the energy current vibrations. I reproduce mentally a virtual operation from the details known to me of anatomic structure. At the same time, I request information about who is going to assist me in this endeavor. More often, I become the physical vehicle which the quasi-forces utilize.

A team of four or five "surgeons" usually attends each patient. From time to time, they communicate with me through internal channels about what they are engaged in and sometimes ask me not to interfere with their task. Depending on their sensitivity or their connection with Higher Forces, some patients can convey the sensations they've experienced, while others are afraid of revealing them, thinking that what happened is more likely a dream or fantasy. In such moments, my palms perceive different information, such as painful signals, pulsations, vibrations, actual mechanical displacements or vibrations of varying frequency, and debilitating cold alternating with burning heat. It is impossible to describe all the sensations.

I conduct similar quasi-operations on myself as well; only in those cases, I imagine myself separated from my body. In the beginning of the operation, I ask for collaboration from the quasi-doctors. Afterwards, it is not mine, but another body being worked on. It is hard to register sensations at such times because I have to listen, on the one hand, to the reactions of the body and what unfolds inside it. On the other hand, I analyze the responses of the nerve endings in the palms, not to mention in the visualization.

It is often difficult to remove the palms from the body, so captivating is the process of self-treatment. I sense clear rolling movements in the area of the stomach, and sometimes cold or heat permeates me. My personal experience tells me that each of us is capable of creating a small miracle. Only one thing is required – will. It is capable of working great wonders, if you only trust in yourself and your quasi-friends. Only you are the creator of your health! If you do not ask, you won't receive the support of the invisible forces surrounding you day and night wherever you are.

Physical signals indicating elevated risk of cancer are a wound or inflammation that is not healing; unusual knots or thickening over and under the skin, especially in the region of lymphatic nodes, mammary ducts, neck, or armpits; various transformations occurring with birthmarks or warts; continuous pains in the area of the stomach, intestine, esophagus; incessant cough; or unending bloody discharges. All demand immediate referral to specialists.

The cause of cancer can always be found if one investigates the previous life of the patient. Cancer results when the previous life of the sick person was inappropriate and there has been prior treatment in this lifetime for another disease with medication or an operation. As soon as the body loses its capacity for resistance, the cancer immediately emerges from its hiding place.

The question of nutrition occupies a special place both in self-healing and in the process of treatment. Its significance is impossible to exaggerate. It is one of the major factors in the treatment of all diseases, without exception. Proper nutrition is one of the weapons in the fight for life by cancer patients that is in the hands of the afflicted themselves. By listening to one's inner voice or subconscious, the patient intuitively can find the necessary elements of nutrition or necessary herbs. This resembles the way wild animals can find the right remedy by themselves.

In a number of cases when the patients requested recommendations on correct nutrition, I directed them to herbologists and dietitians, or to libraries where the patients begin to research their healing nutriments. The main thing is the desire! No one knows the intricacies of your body better than you.

According to both my observations and the observations of oncologists, preference in the diet must be for raw herbal products. The human being is herbivorous. Thus, in cases of cancer, green tea can be very useful. Numerous studies have already established that green tea contains special microelements, aiding not only the removal of radioactive elements, but also the retardation of oncological processes.

Smoked beef or bacon, nitrates, arsenic, asbestos, paraffin, aniline, heavy metals, polyvinyl chloride, and some medications nourish the oncogenes, which promote the onset of cancer. Long-term stress also promotes development of cancer. Japanese scientists have reported that induced abortions seem to promote future tumors not only in the first generation, but for the one after it. It is worthwhile to ponder over these facts!

It is very important to regularly include in the diet a sufficient amount of rough fiber, such as bran, bread baked from coarse-ground flour, vegetables (except potatoes), fruits, and parsley. These products facilitate elimination of many carcinogenic substances as well as toxic by-products of degraded cholesterol. Rough fibers play an important part in the prophylaxis of cancer of the gastrointestinal tract (especially of the large intestine).

Why is it necessary to give preference to raw herbal products? The antioxidants and phytonutrients in them possess anti-tumor fighters. The fibers of the raw food stabilize the microflora of the intestine. Healthy microflora produces substances participating in anti-cancer defenses.

The deficiency of essential and fatty acids, Vitamins E and B_6, makes the body more vulnerable to carcinogens. A good source of essential and fatty acids can be olive, sunflower, and soy oils. Vitamins E and B_6 are contained in unrefined flour and whole-meal bread. Also, Vitamin E is abundant in egg yolk, whole grain flour, while Vitamin B_6 is present in yeast, liver, milk and coarse-grained flour.

Everyone knows that the eastern cuisine is very colorful in its diversity of vegetables, fruits and spices. The phytochemicals contained in them help the body to preserve its form longer. From the diverse groups of carotenoids, which are known for elevating immunity and reducing the chance of cancer, six types were found to be the most effective. The following products contain them: melon, strawberry, squash, red and yellow pepper, peaches, raspberry, mango, carrots and yellow vegetables. Other products that prevent or reduce the risk of cancer are beets, salad greens, broccoli, brussel sprouts or cabbage, tomatoes, beans, nuts (2 - 5 almonds per day) and seeds. To help treat cancer of the uterus, a woman should receive daily about 750 i.u. (international units) of betacarotene, the amount contained in a large carrot, with a teaspoon of oil or sour cream. Lowering the calorie value of the diet slows down cancer development only in animals, not in humans!

Silica plays an important role in both the prevention and treatment of cancer. It is contained in the peels of vegetables and fruits and the outer shell of grains. Therefore, one should not necessarily peel vegetables and fruits.

From one of my readers at **www.quasimir.com**:

"One of my co-workers was diagnosed seven years ago with leukemia. His prognosis was not very good; he was told he had about 6-12 months to live. His physicians informed him of the importance of chemotherapy treatment, which he refused.

The patient decided to seek alternative methods of treatment. He researched the effects of diet comprised of raw fruits and vegetables. In his research, he came across a scientific study done at a nearby village of Chernobyl. The majority of the population located near the nuclear plant explosion had been diagnosed with some form of cancer. However, this one village had very few incidences of cancer. It was later concluded that the people's diet at this nearby village consisted primary of raw/cooked beets. The research scientists hypothesized that eating those cooked beets contributed to the majority of cancer-free population at this nearby village of Chernobyl.

Despite the advice of his physicians, my colleague thus began a strict diet consisting primarily of raw fruits, vegetables, especially beets, and fresh-squeezed juices. His prognosis was getting better. He made it through the first 6 months. Although his physicians warned he may have a relapse, he continued with the diet. Seven years have passed and my co-worker is still with us today.

So, what kinds of minerals and/or vitamins do beets contain that help with the treatment of cancer?
Sincerely, Gail L."

Frequently asked questions about the necessity of the specific diet for some patients reminded me about this wonder vegetable, and so I decided to share the available information concerning red beets with the readers.

Magic Diet

At my parents' house – second to potatoes – red beets were always one of the main vegetables at meals. During my youth, I did not pay any attention to their medicinal quality. Beets only became part of my diet after I have learned about their healing benefits. The Oncology/Hematology Department of the local hospital used beets as an active ingredient in their patient meals because of their miraculous qualities.

The medicinal value of beets was used by such well-known doctors of the distant past as Avicenna, Hypocrite, Galen and Paracelsus. Doctors of Ancient Greece used beet juice to cure fevers, anemia, and diseases of the digestive and lymphatic systems.

The root of the beet contains a large amount of sugar, a small amount of fiber, fat, a large amount of cellulose, pectin, organic, pantothenic and folic acids, many vitamins, various microelements (iron, iodine, calcium, potassium, cobalt, magnesium, manganese, copper, fluorine and zinc), pigments and many other substances.

A beet surpasses many vegetables because it contains amino acids and mineral substances. The beets have a gamma-amino acid, which plays an important role in metabolism.

The use of beets for medicinal purposes has been proven by scientific study. Research from the last decade validated the curative properties of dark-colored red beets.

Betaine and betanin – an albuminous, alkaloid-like substance in the red beet – improve the digestion of food and help to create choline, the substance that increases cell activity in the liver, strengthens the walls of capillaries, decreases cholesterol in the blood and improves the metabolism of fat. Choline readily forms salts, several of which have been used in medicine as lipotropic agents in the treatment of fatty degeneration and hepatic cirrhosis.

As indigestible cellulose, pectin and organic acid contained in the beet travel through the digestive system, they absorb and remove from the body poisonous substances of microbic origin, salts of heavy metals, radioactive isotopes and cholesterol deposits. In addition, these substances in the beets strengthen peristalsis, promotes active secretion of digestive juices and bile. Red beets also promote wound-healing, act as a diuretic, anesthesia, laxative, or anti-inflammatory. Red beets also aid in the lowering of blood pressure.

For medicinal purposes, it is best to use the root of the beet, its juices and its leaves. In case of illnesses of the liver, constipation, digestion, obesity and hypertension, it is recommended to eat 100-150 g. of cooked beets on an empty stomach. One or two tablespoons of beet juice also can be taken before meals. Better effects are achieved when beet juice is diluted with water and other juices. The regular consumption of beet juice rejuvenates the skin. Juice from raw beets or freshly grated beets is richer in vitamins and minerals than juice made from cooked beets. However, cooked beets or cooked beet juice is better for digestion problems. Hungarian physicians recommend drinking beet juice in dozes not more than 100 ml. daily. During my trip to Turkey, I noticed that local residents drink beet juice after they consume meat.

The combination of beet and carrot juices provides phosphorus, sulfur, potassium and other alkaline elements necessary for the human body. This mix of juices also provides plenty of vitamin A. Beta carotene found in vegetables has antioxidant properties, which means it protects cells from the daily toxic damage of oxidation.

Vitamin A helps in the formation and maintenance of healthy teeth, skeletal and soft tissue, mucous membranes and skin. Vitamin A promotes good vision, especially in dim light. It may also help reproduction and lactation. It must be remembered that vitamin A is absorbed by the digestive system only in combination with fat or oil, so mix it with any kind of oil or sour cream, even a very small amount is enough.

In recent years, red beets have been proven to reduce the activity of cancerous cells. In cancer cells, their oxidizing processes are limited while lactic fermentation is increased. The red pigment of the red beet – glucosin-betanin – serves as the substitute for the respiratory enzymes in the cancer cells and inhibiting growth.

To improve their health, some patients need only to take 250 g. of the grated beet or 200-300 g. of the beet juice daily. However, many patients add 1 kg of raw vegetables to their diet as well. In the case of skin cancer, bandages with beet concentrate should be applied several times a day. And it is very good to mix beet juice with carrot juice. Don't forget to put a drop of oil in the mix. Pure beet juice is potent, so two tablespoons are enough on a daily basis.

As a rule, the improvement comes for cancer patients after two or three weeks: the fever is reduced, the patient's weight is increased, sedimentation rate of erythrocytes is decreased, tumor growth is decreased, and the constitution of blood improves. Once the treatment with beets has begun, it is necessary to continue. Stopping treatment may cause a relapse. For best results, eliminate foods containing flour, sugar or red meat.

Blueberries, black currants, St. John's wort and red wine have similar effects on cancerous tumors. However, red beets are more effective. The fresher the beet juice is, the better its effectiveness.

In spite of the miraculous qualities of red beets, you should not assume that this vegetable is the panacea. A diet containing red beets should be used to compliment traditional medical treatment for cancer.

I share the following material which I've accumulated over many years of practice. It might seem absurd to some, but I ask you to read attentively and analyze your own life experiences, and then decide whether or not to agree with me. You may have noticed how members of one family get sick with the same diseases, not necessarily infectious, but seem to be transmitted from one member of the family to another. An ailment appears without apparent reason. If one considers a well-established phenomenon that mental activity is common to the whole human body, not just the brain, then it follows that all cells not only think, but communicate with each other despite the distances that separate them. Therefore, the healthy cells, upon receiving signals from abnormal ones, change their vital rhythm until they come into resonance with the abnormal ones. The telepathic abilities of the cells are easily traced in examining the onset of family oncological problems.

However, do not be frightened! Research has determined that the sick cells affect the healthy ones only if they are under dark conditions. With the visualization of blue or white light, the process reverses: the sick cells die; the healthy ones do not absorb the disease-inducing information, remaining unharmed. Thus it is possible to end communication between the healthy and abnormal cells with the help of a laser beam or the energy impact of the healer.

This part of the chapter I dedicate to all my former patients who always became confused when I advised them, in certain cases, to sleep with a dim light on. This especially relates to spouses, if one of them has the disease. Many couples and many tragedies have passed before my eyes! It can help to have a night-light in the bedroom for those who would like to be on guard for their own health. During all times, their bedrooms should be equipped with a nightlight.

The first person who came to me was a young woman who had experienced confusing sensations. With the help of diagnosis, a pre-cancerous condition of the pancreas was established. She took no preventive measures. After quite some time had elapsed, she asked for my help; this time, cancer was found. All of this caused suspicion on my part. It arose too early. The distance scanning of her husband confirmed my worst fears; he had cancer of the pancreas, but in a more progressive stage than she had. If it were not for the Chernobyl catastrophe, his cancer would not have developed. The refractory cells of the husband were transformed into cancerous ones, and they altered the healthy cells of the wife. It took twelve years for the problem to surface.

Analyzing a multitude of facts about information transmission on the cellular and energy level, I have noted a special significance of photos, pictures, or other modes of reflecting human individuality and its impact on the family. In a number of religions, particularly Judaism, a temporal record of the human face is forbidden in all devices of the arts. Where ancient cultural values endure in Africa, it is considered an enormous crime to depict human beings in art. From the perspective of energy information, our portraits retain forever the information not only about us as human beings, but also about our genetic karmic potential. It is the accumulator of all transformations that have passed, are passing, or are expected in the future. As a repository of the info-energy, any drawn impression participates in the exchange with other informational sources, whether living or not. If a portrait carries information about such diseases as cancer, psychological disorders, or other afflictions, it will affect all that surrounds it!

Relatives are prone to this special influence because they tend to keep their own portraits as well as those of whom they share blood ties, in full view in the same spot throughout their lives. An interrupted exchange occurs on that subtle level which cannot be registered by conventional methods. Genetically close subjects are predisposed towards informational infection. Their ultra-weak light emissions affect those most like them without particular effort. The conclusion from this is that it is necessary to keep photos or impressions of the dead separate from living subjects due to oncological or karma-genetic reasons. It may sound strange, but if you think about it in depth, you might find an incident that supports this possibility from your own experience.

This recalls the feelings that we get when we find ourselves in a house where several people have died from the same disease. The house, which is infected energetically, continues to afflict the inhabitants. It is for this reason that the custom of burning or burying the dead with his apparel has come into existence.

I will never forget how, during the evening after we buried my mother, after all the relatives had gone, my father called my sister and me into his room. What he said made us restless. In his family's tradition, all belongings worn by the dead must be burned. My father was present while things to be discarded were chosen. It may be hard to imagine our state of mind when, living in our parents' house, we were ritually sacrificing into the fire the things that retained the scent of our mother's body. At the wish of my father, the same ritual was performed on the day of his own burial. The feeling of inexplicable lightness that permeated us at the completion of this ancient custom is preserved in my memory. It was energetically pure inside our house after the rituals.

These traditions remain in many cultures, beginning from ancient Egyptian times, the records of which are preserved. Each culture has its own methods of cleansing the rooms of negative information accrued throughout a certain period of time, and practices range from dispelling vapors of special herbs to particular procedures of purification.

From time to time, I have to ask my patients and their acquaintances where they live or where their beds are located in cases of protracted recovery. The questions are far from idle. Those who are familiar with biopathogenic zones do not have to read through this material, but for those who are interested, I will try to give a general summary. All who have dogs or cats know that their little friends prefer certain places of rest rather than others. According to folk belief, when one is moving into a new house or apartment, it can be advisable to let a cat in first, and at the spot where it stations itself, put a bed.

The problem of geopathic zones was known centuries ago. At the time of Peter the Great, every builder had the ability to locate geopathic zones, also called "rotten places." One of the oldest methods of finding a place for a new town was described by ancient Roman builder Vitrivius Pollio in his book "De Archtektura". In the place chosen for construction, people established a pasture. Later they killed all the animals and carefully examined all their internal organs. If livers of these animals were damaged, the builders looked for another place to build the town.

The modern research of "holy" or "rotten place" started in the 19th century by German doctors who began paying attention to the phenomena of "cancer houses." Residents of these houses were dying one after another from oncological diseases.

As verified by modern research, the Earth's surface is covered by an energy net, like a geographical map with latitudes and meridians traced on it. Their location is somewhat different from the geographical one, for the position of the lines is in a state of perpetual change. This is called the geobiological net, and it is rather wide. It stretches from north to south at intervals of two meters, and from east to west at intervals of two and a half meters. In addition to the geobiological net, there are also splits in the Earth's crust where one can find a clear deficiency in the power of the magnetic field. Places where the lines intersect are called poles. They can be either positive or negative. The negative poles or zones are called geopathic due to their ability to cause illness, i.e., physical changes in health of those people who have resided near those poles for a long time.

The immune system of the human body resists their impact. However, with the passing of time, it becomes harder and harder to perform the job of supporting the energy self-regulation of the body, when the intensity of the geopathic rays does not weaken and the energy resources of the body are being sapped.

From time to time, notices appear in the press which describe with bewilderment a plethora of cancer cases in people who have recently moved into a particular house or apartment house or are working in a particular building. An elevated frequency of cancer is found both in urban areas located within the boundaries of various extra-knots and centers and in the area of powerful and extended zones. These zones produce an extremely unfavorable ecological effect amounting to a high probability of various diseases in people and animals who remain there for a long time. These diseases include failure of cardiovascular, nervous, digestive, and other systems, arthritis, memory loss, rheumatism, asthma, neurosis, and benign and malignant tumors.

In the rooms through which geopathic zones and their intersections pass, there is a prevalence of those affected by psychological disorders, brain tumors, stomach cancer, lung cancer, and other problems. The presence of such zones at places of work, an office or business, along with other causes, leads to reduction in the productivity of work, and possibly reduces the quality of the resulting product.

The opinion that we can adapt to the conditions created by geopathic zones after having been there for a long time is erroneous. Life in these zones provokes the onset of disease, especially cancer. The contribution of geopathic zones to the onset of cancer comprises as much as 50%, according to some scientific estimates. While this is not such good news, the knowledge allows us to take precautions.

There are a number of methods from ancient times for locating geopathic zones. One of them is use of a grapevine or a T-shaped metallic indicator. The T-shaped indicator is assembled from smooth metallic wire with a diameter around two mm or about one eight of an inch, at a 90 degree angle in proportion of 1:2. The best material is polished steel, the worst – aluminum or copper. One does not have to possess heightened sensitivity to determine the location of the geopathic region in the living area. During a perambulation across a room with a T-shaped indicator, it will turn in certain places. If, throughout several experiments, the turning of the frame repeats at the same spot, then be assured that you have located a geopathic zone.

Not long ago I had a dream in which Rene, the mother of a former patient, was asking for help for her son, Dan. For some reason, I told Rene that Dan has nothing threatening him, but he is upset about something. I advised her to relocate Dan's bed and desk to another place in his bedroom. I also gave her a copy of this part of my book, concerning geopathic zones. Later I called her and discussed my dream. To my surprise, Rene told me that Dan had moved his bed to another place two days before I had my dream, and that she had also had a dream about me at that time. We both were struck by this apparent coincidence. I asked Rene for a description of her son's bedroom, and then recommended a new location for Dan's bed and desk. Our dreams sometimes tell or advise us more than we can normally expect from sources in reality. Harken to your dreams and you will be set in the right direction.

Life, from birth until death, is a chain of continued decisions, and the knowledge that results from them must be grasped before it's too late. Faith in one's personal mission in existence will enhance all one's attempts to find the answers to overcoming sickness of the body or the mind. Whoever is interested in reading material relating to this subject and its ideas will always find a way to expand his/her knowledge.

Chapter VII

WHY SUCH
A FATE?

Remember that you are an actor in a drama, of such a part as it may please the master to assign you, for a long time or for a little as he may choose. And if he wills you to take the part of a poor man, or a cripple, or a ruler, or a private citizen, then you may act that part with grace! For to act well the part that is allotted to us, that indeed is ours to do, but to choose it is another's.

—Epistetus

Chance

The day is bright as light in us

To show the way that we must follow
We try to walk the mystic path
To reach the destiny of ours
The light that guides us in a day
That light which brightens way at night
There are the ways that lead us down
There are those ways that raise us higher
We make decisions on the moment
To choose the path that's made for us
Sometimes that path deceives us all
It is the mystery of life we love
Not knowing what's in front
To take a chance to make a choice.

N. Madorsky

One morning a group of women came to our house unexpectedly. My mother spoke for a few minutes with the women, and then gladly signed their petition. The petition was to be presented to a judge. Later she told my father that people from our neighborhood were defending their favorite doctor. The doctor was persecuted for performing an abortion, illegal after World War II. A couple of years later the doctor came back to the hospital to work. The husband of the patient was the Chief of Police. Years later the same doctor was with me when I was in labor with my second child. She was one of the best doctors in town. The trial of innocent people with medical backgrounds still haunts my memories from childhood. Since that time I learned how to guard myself.

My gift as a healer springs from my childhood. When I was five years old I healed myself of my wounds inflicted by a piece of glass. Ever since I have practiced healing with my own unique techniques, using the power of mind, dreams, maps of palms, Eastern philosophy of the art of healing, nutrition and "healing touch." I treated minor aches, burns, pains, wounds and nervous exhaustion on the subconscious level. I was always amazed at my ability, but experience instilled confidence in my own gift. Instinctively trying to be accepted by others, I protected myself from their skepticism. Despite the strength of my soul and the power of my spiritual healing gift, my hour had not yet come. My gift had to be cultivated. Among my relatives, I was called either a "family" or "cats" doctor or completely ignored. I occasionally predicted the future accurately; not due to my will, but to that of fate. As is said, one cannot argue with fate. Relatives used my talents, but I generally tried to keep my healing and spiritual abilities to myself, not attracting attention, as many had done in my home country Belarus.

I was about six or seven years old when my mother was sick with erysipelas, a skin disease which affected her nose. Suffering from her affliction, she went again and again to the doctor. Finally the doctor informed her, through the nurse, to find a "witch doctor," as he did not know how to fight such a malady. A "witch doctor" was found without delay. I remember my mother being treated, lying in a dark room with a red cloth over her face. Science now confirms of the usefulness of darkening the room and the utilization of red light, but this was not so years ago. This incident was mentioned more than once in our family circle.

While I was maturing spiritually, I completed nursing courses and worked as a nurse for one year in a children's clinic. I attempted to enter medical school in the formerly Soviet Belarus. Though passing the entrance exam, I was not admitted. However, I was not upset. I even sensed relief in the depth of my soul as I went on with my life.

The next year I left for the Ukraine. There I entered college in Kiev to study electrical engineering. This was a tribute to my father, who was an engineer and had taught us to view the world through a philosophically analytical perspective. "Take nothing on faith," he said. "Verify everything before accepting it."

My father descended from a noble family of Belarus which after October Revolution was stripped of everything it had. The members of the family tried very hard to conceal their heritage and spoke of it only among themselves. This gave my father an opportunity to finish college and to acquire an administrative position in a ministry, while others entered the engineering field. He also, proved to be a very good inventor. He wrote for major national technical magazines and newspapers. I illustrated some of my father's articles. We spent many hours together on research. I learned a lot from his advice and knowledge.

My mother was an accounting supervisor in a large company until she quit her job to rear her children. I am very proud of her choice despite all the difficulties resulting from having one income with a large family. She was an open book of ancient wisdom received from her grandmother. My mother was only three years old when her mother and twin sister were killed. Her spirit and love for people, despite having a hard life, gave me strength and courage. She was an example for how to survive during difficult times. Once, when already a parent, I asked her a very important question. It was about my older brother, who vanished or was killed during World War II. He was only six years old. My brother was only two years old when he was sent with his nanny to a village for summer vacation in May of 1941 because my mother was pregnant with the second child. My memory still holds pictures of traveling by bus with mother to this village, looking for him years after the war. People from the community never told her a German family adopted him. He was a beautiful boy with blond hair and lovely blue eyes, like his father. The German authorities kidnapped Aryan-looking children from occupied lands. My parents tried not to discuss his disappearance with us. What was my mother's attitude toward Germans? Her response shocked me and was one of the greatest lessons for me. With a deep sadness in her eyes she said: "Not every German is an awful person." My parents lost not only their son in the war, but many relatives as well. They always believed that he was still alive. This story is included in case my brother is still alive and has a chance to read this book. He will feel our connections. He has the same gift as his siblings, our mother and I do, spirituality and sensitivity toward people surrounding us. If I found him I would know how to identify my brother: he has an unusual, unseen feature on his body.

Years have since passed. Behind me is a career as a nurse, engineer and professor, a serious and deep appraisal of my talents, and a conviction of the power of my destiny in this world. The experience of dealing with people and technology allows me to treat the physical body successfully, to influence the emotional state of the patient, and to investigate the accrued material shifted by the screen of my personal impressions and the feelings of my patients.

Rearing my own children, I confronted the frequent realities of childhood illnesses, and often employed my healing gift granted by nature. Can anyone forget the episodes of the early life of his or her children? When one of my sons cried, I placed my healing hands on his stomach and a miracle took place. He would fall asleep in a moment.

When I read in a book, magazine or newspaper about some outstanding healer, I thought that the article dealt with a genius of its own kind when compared to me, a self-starter. I had no opportunity to determine whether we were equally successful in treating people's ailments, despite the difference in the methods of treatment. I knew that in every town and village there lived special people who could help at times when doctors were powerless to do so.

I went through many personal cataclysms before I ventured to confess that I had a spiritual gift. The fear of recognition as being gifted – left over from the age of medieval persecution – abated, and I dared to declare aloud to the cosmos: "I was born to render assistance to those who haven't completed their mission in this world. I ask that those who wish for and are ready to struggle for the completion of their mission find me."

On the 25th anniversary of my marriage to my husband, I invited around forty people to our wedding anniversary party. Among my friends was my legal consultant, Terry. She had recently undergone an operation for ovarian cancer. In all the years I knew her, Terry had never appeared to be ill. She was doing aerobics, playing tennis, and leading an active social and professional life. The disease surfaced quite unexpectedly during a vacation cruise.

In spite of the traveling involved and sweltering summer heat, as well as anxiety over forthcoming chemotherapy, Terry attended my anniversary celebration. As I was saying goodbye to her and her husband, I saw tears in his eyes. Moved by an unconscious impulse, I offered my help. I tried to explain to both of them that I possess a gift to alleviate suffering and accelerate recovery, even in cases where modern medicine is powerless. Due to their symptomatic rather than wholistic approach to treatment, some physicians break the ancient oath of Hippocrates: "The most important thing is to do no harm."

In conclusion I added, "It wouldn't make things worse, but perhaps it would help." Why I offered is a mystery to me. This happened spontaneously and with only one desire on my part – to ease the suffering of a person dear to me. At that moment, I feared that our relationship might never be the same.

Years ago, Terry acted as a volunteer hostess for our family, using her social connections. She helped us out of a sense of community obligation rather than for personal interest. Two traits were always in conflict within her – the positive, when she was well-disposed, and the negative, which manifested itself in times of despair. She was the mirror of her parents. If we had not stayed one night at her house, many years ago, her destiny would probably have turned in a very different direction.

The struggle for Terry's life began with the greatest struggle of all – the battle between life and death. Working with all my heart, the life energy flowed through my hands and refilled the stores of energy in the body of the patient, previously enervated by disease. This was the only chance for survival, because there was no time left for an alternative treatment.

Gradually, Terry took a renewed confidence in God deeply into her heart. During the sessions, she began using my recommended visual and breathing exercises, which contributed to her improvement.

The fight for Terry's life involved the reconciliation of separate cultures, views, different thinking and attitudes toward human values, medical suggestions and demands. We both achieved spiritual growth, which under different circumstances would have taken many years to complete. In this battle there were no losers, only winners. Both of us gained something; both of us lost something. We both realized that our relationship would never be the same. Time judges us and ranks everything according to its merit. What mattered was that her life has been preserved for an indefinite length of time. For how long? It does not depend upon me. Everything is now in the hands of Terry. She wants to make the most of the time she has been left, and so far she has. Now she is running for a government office. I admire her courage and optimism like others who know her.

Before the start of each session, we said a prayer together in which we asked our Lord to aid in Terry's treatment and affirmed that only she was responsible for the process of recovery. Thus she became used to her personal responsibility for her health and the blessing from above. At every healing session I silently initiated my own prayer to God.

Revelation*

Oh, our God! Oh, our Lord! Oh, our Creator!

Oh, our Father! Oh, our Master!

Let You be forever at the heavens of the Universe!

Let Your name be sacred in the memory of our descendants!

Let Your reign stay undisturbed forever and ever!

Let Your word be eternal in the earthly and heavenly realms!

Let there be Your blessing upon all our noble acts!

Let there be Your forgiveness for our debts and trespasses!

Let there be Your permission upon the forgiveness of our debtors!

Let there be Your favor upon the protection from our temptations!

Let there be Your mercy for our sins!

Let there be Your will for the deliverance of us

from devilish snares!

Let there be all that was said and written with

Your will forever and ever!

Amen!

---

*Prayer of R. Madorsky

Before going to sleep, try to shine light through your own body, as though you are doing an X-ray of all your body parts. The results will appear shortly. I perform this on myself as well.

From time to time during the session, I ask the patient to scan his organs with visualized white light, persuading him that he is capable of locating his own imminent problems. In all cases this self-analysis works accurately. Be your own diagnostician. You can be your own physician.

The recommended colors of the light currents vary during the visualization, depending on to which organ they are directed and which disease they are targeting. When working with cancer patients, I advise them to visualize streams of blue light on the cancer cells during therapy and in their free time. The blue light suppresses the activity of tumor cells. In case the patient is unable to visualize blue light during cancer treatment, I ask him to imagine white light. Generally, it is better to use white light in all other cases because its spectrum is composed of all seven major colors of the rainbow. In a state of depression, however, visualizing yellow light is recommended.

This pivotal time spent in fighting Terry's disease brought me to a crossroads, whether to continue my professional career as an engineer, or completely devote myself to improving people's health. The choice was made for me from the urgency of others seeking help and gave me no time for reflection. My patients appeared as though by divine direction.

Terry mentioned to her friend Bonnie that I was treating her. Bonnie had been diagnosed with inoperable lung cancer. During my first meeting with Bonnie, I had decided that I would not work with her, as I was uncomfortable in her house. My decision seemed strange to me, and was not my usual way of reacting. When I came to Bonnie's house, I felt like a fish washed ashore by a sudden wave. I could neither inhale nor exhale. This was a warning that danger was present and I must be watchful. So often I have gone ahead with the spirit of the researcher taking control and against my better judgment, I visited Bonnie. During the first few sessions, Bonnie shared her background and family tree, but soon our meetings became fights for the spirit and the body. It was hard to imagine that Bonnie, a conservative believer in traditional medicine with an education in a health profession, could seek salvation from a healer. But she knew that there was no hope for a medical miracle. And there was also the awareness that her mother had also embraced natural healing, and she was over 90.

I had to overcome considerable stubbornness in Bonnie, her immovable faith in the medical establishment and her fear that someone would find out that she was exploring alternative healing to survive. Her belief in the authority of the established medical world gradually dissipated. Yet she had such self-absorbing, false pride! Bonnie tried to conceal the name of her oncologist, well known for his publications in the scientific community, by crossing out references to him in the laboratory reports she gave to me. Our healing sessions were kept secret, not only from her friends, but also from her relatives. Her fear was comparable to that of individuals during the Dark Ages when thinking contrary to the church-imposed dogma was condemned as heresy.

It was not easy for me to work with Bonnie. But a patient is a patient. He or she must be treated. Months later Bonnie's battle was over and she, like hundreds of others who had been healed, enjoyed life once more.

Cancer patients differ somewhat from patients with other diseases. Many instantly panic, often accepting the message about their ill health as a divine punishment. Only a few start looking for alternative ways of deliverance from the disease beyond those offered by traditional medicine. This novel path represents a victory over one's prejudices and the personal worship of medical luminaries. Bonnie gained her first victory against inoperable lung cancer when she asked for help via unconventional methods and planned to use both methods of treatment simultaneously.

When considering general human health and cancer, in particular, the important aspects to search for are the cause of oncological disorders and the ways of preventing their development. At least, determining methods of early diagnosis provides timely support to the body as well as to the soul.

Each new patient has a particular destiny, but all are bound by something in common. The ways they find me are inscrutable, surrounded by mystery and chance. The first meeting often appears miraculous; however, there is no miracle. A predetermined chain of interrelated events, meetings and the environment makes it possible for them to reach me. Their impressions of our initial contact vary from amazement to placidity, similar to an arrival on a long awaited shore.

I encountered Gail at the office of a Chinese doctor who maintained a herbal health shop in a large store. Gail had used the Chinese doctor's services for more than ten years. This time, however, she came to the doctor with a really big problem – a tumor had been found in her breast. I was there because my patient, Greg, a pharmacist, did not want to discontinue his strong medication, which was retarding the healing process. I wanted him to substitute the chemical products with natural ones.

Gail was in tears. Upon learning of her problem, I gave her my card. I encouraged her to attend one of my seminars. At a seminar on healing arts, she signed up for healing sessions with me, although her doctor had advised an operation on her breast. The sessions that followed, allowed me to stop pre-cancerous changes in her uterus that discovered. An operation proved unnecessary since a benign breast tumor had been detected. I knew some of her problem came from her tension. Gail is still employed in a stressful, high-powered job. I worry that her future is at risk because she does not slow down and enjoy life.

Everything is as old as the world itself. The difference is that some truly remarkable healers try to share their secrets with their followers so their students will not repeat their mistakes but would learn from them. Others, of less ethical nature, take advantage of the demand for such literature and discreetly copy and distort the original meaning embodied in the sources of Nature.

One of the ancient ways of looking for the innate healers is palmistry. On the left palm of those marked by God with the gift of healing, one can find certain distinctive signs which not only show who he is, but also convey how he is protected from external interference.

What can one do in such cases and whom can one trust? My opinion, which I try to convey to those who care, is to trust your inner voice. It is your best friend and adviser, assistant and doctor. Your inner voice, your subconscious, your second "I" knows all. It is connected with the Universal information field. Have you ever thought that the Universal Mind knows everything, and one must only be able to connect to it in order to request the necessary information?

The energy fields we generate travel with great velocity, and their magnitudes have been measured by physicists. Imagine you just thought about something; your idea then no longer belongs to you, the source – it goes into orbit and is stored in the permanent memory of the Universal Mind. It has been proven that a thought is material with a mass equal to $10^{(-35)} - 10^{(-32)}$ grams and, from the moment of its origin, exists independently of its source. Let me offer you some general advice: "Think before you formulate a plan."

Everyone knows that the saying to "have a good or an evil eye" (the folk phrase) is a phenomenon confirmed by life. If, at some point, you created or experienced an impulse in your brain, its energy, even despite your will, can be directed toward someone or something. Positive or negative impulses can strengthen or weaken the energy field around organs or systems or the whole human body or some object. "If you think, then do it with positive inclination. If you can't, turn to thoughts about Nature."

This true incident happened to me many years ago. I gave birth to a third child and was at home with my kids when I burned my left hand with boiling corn oil. I suffered indescribable pain. I could not cry since I was trying to focus and use all my medical knowledge to treat my hand, and I could not leave my kids to go to the hospital. I was desperately looking for help. An hour later my mom came home and I showed her my hand. She looked in my eyes, as though nothing happened, and calmly told me to grease my hand with cold corn oil. Within seconds the pain subsided completely. It was miracle to me like others I experienced with my mother. She had a great gift to heal people but never revealed it outside the family. Everybody who knew her told me about her ability to heal people's souls and that she had a "good eye."

It happened during the Second World War when she had been evacuated to Kazakhstan. There, she had a second child. She had malaria and was nearly dying. In the area where she stayed neither medicine nor doctors could be found. My father was at war. The owner of the house, a Kazakh woman, recommended that my mother drink a cup of her own urine. This cup of urine saved my mother's life. She fully recovered from malaria. She told her children this and similar stories about the healing power of Nature many times in her life.

From time to time, I have been tested not only by my Higher Power, but also by curious people. My colleague, Richard, came to me once to determine whether I was a good healer. The result of this positive evaluation of my abilities so astonished him that he not only began to attend sessions, but spent time with me in profound conversations about metaphysics and healing methods. This useful exchange of experience led me to consider writing this book. Richard became my patient, student, and follower, and started to refer other healers and people in need to me for treatment. Although Richard had studied more than seven years in an East Coast school of mystics and had come in contact with many well-known healers during those years, he knew for the first time what it meant to be a natural born healer, rather than a healer by professional training.

Chapter VIII

KNOW
THYSELF

*We know nothing important. In the essentials
we are still as wholly a mystery to ourselves
as Adam was to himself.*
—Booth Tarkington

Spring

The trees are coming back to life

The birds are coming back from south
There is a music in the air it is a life of living time
The time has come to let it go
To go somewhere never been before
To have the things that never had
To live the life I never lived
It is the time to have it done
The air is filled with song of life
My life is not by choice of mine
This is that time to change it all
The birds are in the sky of time
To be the life of dreams in time
The spring is here and life begins again
I'll be the one with world to live the life.

N. Madorsky

Who is endowed with healing abilities? Everyone has innate curative powers to help oneself at some level, but not everyone acknowledges, accepts or chooses to use these kinds of gifts. Also, not everyone has the special gift to heal others. This gift comes with God's guidance, ancient wisdom and bears a price. When a new soul is born, God sends this soul on a special mission. This is a mystery of Nature that no one has yet unraveled. Still we have learned how to find those special people, both due to external attributes and due to the types of signals they release. There are only a few healers with a clearly expressed, fully developed talent. May God grant you chance in meeting such a person when you need a healer.

Special attention must be given to the spiritual maturity of the healer. If the potential healer is very young, he is not usually allowed to perform healing practices until reaching the age of 30, according to unwritten laws of the Universe. The reasons for this are immature physical development, incomplete formation of the energy centers or chakras through which the contact with the earthly and cosmic forces occurs, and also the absence of sufficient life experience to battle negative influences of people, nature and society.

For example, the practice of KABBALA – the mystical movement in Judaism – is not allowed before reaching the age of 42, and only when one has family and children! This strict limitation has meaning, if you devote yourself to the service of humanity. This must be the law of all who enter the path of the noble healing arts, which are inexpressible in their harshness and psychological toll. Otherwise, disaster is inevitable for both the practitioner and the afflicted.

At one conference, involving the healing arts of healers, I met an 18-year old girl accompanied by her mother. The mother, answering my question about why her daughter was there, told me she possesses the capacity to heal and had already helped many. The unnatural paleness of the young healer was noticeable. I sensed that her life was already advancing towards its completion – she was no longer alive in this world. Despite warnings of danger from practicing at a young age, she was proceeding due to the encouragement of her mother. It is only a question of time until the girl will have to pay. The desire to learn from one's own mistakes sometimes ends tragically. I again remind you about the indisputable laws proved throughout the ages.

Why I have been endowed with this gift and its meaning, I resign to God's inscrutable purpose. I recall how I have diagnosed people in a moment, people, who passed my way through apparent coincidence, anticipating the trouble that had already woven its web around them. I sometimes feel overwhelmed by my intuition about the health of those who talk with me. To escape, I seek new horizons; novel, fresh topics to divert my interest. Recently I wished to explore how the correlation of past and present can influence what lies ahead, and perhaps turn it in a favorable direction. It contradicts human nature to be enslaved by the past. This leads to degradation of individuality in both the spiritual and physical dimensions.

After meeting and speaking with numerous healers, I have discovered that many of them have obtained their gift from ancestors or from some merit in previous lives. However, others experienced physical or psychological traumas in their youth, and overcame them, through their own will. Any trial of fate develops will and grows strength of character and identity, uncovering the gift of healing. The incidents which I have confronted in my practice confirm the common presence of some tragic event in the lives of those gifted with superior healing talents. There is even much written about the "wounded healer." I tried, on the basis of experiences of other healers, to find additional events that had changed my life. From my early childhood, I recalled a significant episode.

I was five or six years old and was lying in a hospital with an infectious strep throat. This was not my first time in the hospital as a visitor, so I felt quite comfortable. In the evening I was to receive a penicillin injection. I suddenly felt a frantic fear when shown a huge needle. I remember how I crawled out of the room where the injection was to be made, crying and dragging my left leg behind me. Around me, others were celebrating the New Year. Some years later, seeing the same type of needle in the office of an ear-nose-throat practitioner, I understood and was horrified about the evil New Year's trick that the nurses had played on me.

In reality, all truly chosen healers try to conceal their gifts and do not discuss them with others, to avoid attracting attention; for nobody knows what is waiting for them tomorrow, although sometimes healers communicate with other healers. The former physician, Nat, cured a terminally ill patient with healing where medical professionals had failed. As a result of this discovery, he began to use his abilities to predict the future. Without prescribing medication, Nat told his patients what needed to be changed to be healed. His relatives, being physicians, put him on psychotic drugs, considering him insane, thus ruining his career and family life. The doctors completed what his relatives had started by placing him for some time in an institution. In this case, Nat made a tragic mistake. He began revealing his newly-acquired abilities, without giving thought to the time or place.

I wonder whether those marked by God are always allowed to cure? What is the payoff for access to energy and to the Universal knowledge? When in our lives do we receive instructions for healing? Is there any connection between the natural healer and the invisible side – the Quasiworld – that attracts subtle forces to grasp the mysteries of the universe?

Here we suddenly see the balance of justice; on the one side, the gift, on the other, retribution and the greatest positive energy balanced hand-in-hand with tragedy. Instinctively having the abilities to foresee events, I have tried to avoid them and, therefore, I chose the way towards healing. All my life I've protected and cared about my loved ones – the lineage must be preserved and multiplied. For the sake of this, we are given life. We, the healers, being occupied with the present, prepare for the future. Thus, the present proceeds from the past and leads to the future.

People should be more interested in the present time because this provides the chance to fulfil their missions. I think that every good deed is repaid one hundredfold. Nothing passes without a trace. The law of Nature works accurately – it is the law of the preservation of energy. If you make an effort to help, it will come back in another form or dimension; if you take someone's energy by bringing on a disaster, the retribution will arrive sooner or later. I am not uncovering anything new, but I am simply repeating the truth, known to us from our forefathers.

Ancient "Agni-Yoga" wisdom teaches that we must embrace the future. The venom of the past, the so-called absorption into the past, might cause the karmic claims to awaken. To grow spiritually, don't dwell on your negative past. Our force multiplies when we carry our consciousness into the future. It is no use to renew the old vibrations... So we advise you, especially now, to carry your consciousness into the future, and thus, avoid many aspects of previous existences.

This thought is very interesting. Nevertheless, without the foundation of the past, one cannot build the future. It is what happens in the process of healing as well.

Everything is much more complicated than it seems. Only those in good health between the ages of 30 and 50 can start to practice healing arts. This is the Universal law. Ideally, women should begin the healing practice only after menopause because of the interference of Universal energies. Healers have to be careful with energy channeling while having health problems. Healers sometimes neglect their own health while caring for others. Some who have acquired "diplomas" consider the path of the healer easy and quick towards material welfare. Unfortunately, this assumption is an illusion.

We do not have sufficient knowledge about why some people are allowed to comfortably engage in healing or shamanism, while others "pay" for this at great expense. It is quite possible that the answers to such questions are hidden in so-called past lives – in the experience and knowledge which we contribute from one existence to the next. It almost resembles the caste system in India. From life to life, one is ordained to heal, and for each transgression from one's mission, one has to carry burdens in another field, which is nothing like what one can imagine. Therefore, one starts to heal often in one's mature years with a call from the heart, which says: "Hurry up, time cannot wait – the payoff is coming."

Once I received a telephone call from someone wishing to have a session with me. The appointment was scheduled, but no one came. In a year's time, fate brought us face to face. I encountered an exhausted woman and, not clearly knowing why, I offered her assistance. When I gave her my name, she mentioned that she had called me to make an appointment, but never kept it. My diagnosis showed a disruption in her energy system. After a short session, I was able to stop the destructive process. I found out this woman had learned the art of healing others and the time for restitution had come. Those teaching this particular method had forgotten that healing is more than hand movements and techniques. What really matters is who is carrying out the process of healing and whether he has a mission from above. At the end of the session, I warned her about the seriousness of the situation and the need to stop the practice of healing others, to which she replied that she liked it. Since she chose not to stop healing others, her protective shield will continue to weaken. Everyone has free will. After many years, I learned to restrain my inner impulses. It took time and effort before I learned to say "NO" when my mind wanted to say "YES."

Some healers attain rapid and astonishing results in such disorders as headaches and muscle pains or gastrointestinal problems. In most cases, these disorders can be cured simply by the wish of the individual and do not require special gifts from the healer. Our human bodies have wonderful healing systems. However, some healers gain reputations by treating large number of patients who do not require much physical or spiritual strength on the part of the healers. Those healers leave behind the most complicated conditions, the ones which are frequently connected with changing lifestyles, spiritual values, genetics or karma. The real healing of the body is connected with the renewal of human spirit, and this super-objective is not feasible for a weakened organism nor for every healer.

My restless soul prepared me for a prickly way even in my healing practice: encounters with sick people with diseases that do not lend themselves to immediate cure, but require long-term treatment, with continual self struggle, enriching one's knowledge and restoring one's spirit.

The majority of serious diseases stem from energy origins in previous generations and past lives. Through genetic information, diseases are carried on to descendants as lessons. I often wonder why this mission to save people who are not supposed to be alive by ordinary medicine was bestowed on me. Why does some particular person find his way to me, and why is he starting to fight for his life? What has forced others to give up their struggle without even starting? There are always more questions than answers.

Finding the primary cause of disease is a heroic deed, demanding courage to reconsider not just one's spiritual and life values but also one's conviction in the face of truth. All of this, in the end, leads to the awareness of primary causes and the search for answers to questions posed by the sick body, which calls for significant spiritual transformation.

Everyday I receive a lesson for my own mind and body. While using my gift at full strength, my view and perception of the world changes, leading to partial resignation from worldly pleasures to feelings, in some sense, of loneliness amongst others. The feelings resemble the proverb, "Stranger among your own people and at home with strangers."

All my life, I tried to discover and analyze myself, my soul, my mind, and my body. What I have struggled to understand, starting from my childhood, is my feeling of inner loneliness, even among my brothers and sisters, in school, in college, at work ... I remember sitting in the garden, asking the Higher Power about my mission, and receiving a vivid impression: loneliness. Recently, after reading articles by Dr. Bernard Segal, author of *Love, Medicine & Miracles*, I attended his seminar to ask a few questions. As part of the workshop, I made a sketch of myself standing alone on the river shore.

The feeling of loneliness, I think, is common to all deeply connected with the spiritual world. I recall a scene from my childhood. My mother was sitting near the window in deep study; the gaze of her pensive eyes was unconsciously directed outside the window. With whom was she communicating at that moment? I do not know. Why did we naturally respect her moments of privacy? I only know that in any particular moment I can disconnect from outside negative disturbances. The same contemplative trait as my mother had I have as well. I do not know for sure to which information source my brain is connecting at those moments, but I know clearly that, after such short periods of absence, I feel more focused and ready for further life experiences.

Those who have difficulty separating from the outside world can develop such skills through meditation, which requires a rigorous self-discipline to develop oneself. Self-absorption into a hypnotic state allows people to endure the difficult times in their lives and can help them in making important decisions. The ability to instantly relax physically, to doze off, whether one is in a plane, bus, or the backyard, is one of the attributes of healers.

I remember one vivid episode from my childhood. I was writing or sketching with my left hand, and nobody was trying to correct me. I felt free. Then, at school, on the first day, a teacher was standing over me. She was telling me something in a strict manner, requesting me to use my right hand. But then, there was a complete void. Probably those were the most difficult years for me wherein, on the one side, the old Soviet school system tried to change me, forcing me to work with my right hand, while on other side, I was a girl with a strong, independent character, which nobody could alter. How I managed to adjust and survive an elementary school in such conditions, I do not remember, and I do not even want to think any more about it. I still write with my right hand. The rest has been done by my left hand, from drafting to basketball. My mother later told me that I wanted neither to write nor read, although I had gone to school with some prior knowledge of these things. When there was no constant control by a teacher, my hands fulfilled their responsibilities as destiny had ordained. So my first experience of internal struggle was completed, forging my will and teaching me a lot.

Many years later, after leaving Russia and crossing the ocean, I noticed that when working with scissors, I used my right hand. This came as a shock to me. The transformation occurred quite naturally, and now I have no doubts that currently the motor centers of both my brain hemispheres are working equally now. Science confirms that left-handed healers are more powerful than right-handed, but I am leaving this explanation to them.

During healing sessions I use both hands, although the energy-transmission of the left palm is more expressive, which is often noticed by my patients. This does not play any special part but makes me comfortable during the process of healing and offers the chance to manipulate energy well with both palms, separately and together.

Gifted healers born with paranormal abilities have distinctive marks on their hands. The ticket for healing cannot be attained only through learning and the acquisition of a certificate to practice. The Higher Power chooses a person and gives him or her protection. Without this permission, it is not beneficial to practice healing, because both the sick and the healer suffer. Did you know that the average life expectancy is much lower for a doctor than for other professionals? The chosen people also need to learn how to protect themselves and care for themselves before healing others.

In all historical eras, there has existed a certain closed circle of initiates, which no one attempted to penetrate with a corrupt goal. Nature has filters. The knowledge was transmitted from generation to generation, and only rarely was there an outsider. Only God knows why those seeking help receive his energy or counsel through his messenger, the healer. The factors affecting the character formation of the healer are the cultural, ethical, religious or atheistic environments in which he has matured, how he was brought up, the level of his education, his country of birth, and his social relationships – almost everything impacts his development. Finally, it becomes apparent that one needs only to be chosen, and the knowledge will come at the right time. Seek your own way for guidance in this infinite world.

Speaking about the personal qualities of the healer and his or her mission and selection, I would like to persuade every reader that such qualities manifest themselves in all people but are not realized with sufficient clarity by all.

The process of developing healing abilities is a life-long process of self-discovery and self-knowledge. The earlier one discovers the source of one's own healing energy, the brighter and healthier he or she will become. When one follows the path where talent lies, one's life will be more fruitful. If one seeks, one will find.

Chapter IX

FORGOTTEN

—

RECOVERED

A word is not a crystal, transparent and unchanging; it is the skin of a living thought may vary greatly in color and content according to the circumstances and time in which it is used.

— Justice Oliver Wendell Holmes

The Times Is

Time does not wait for anyone

It runs with might of strongest wind
It is the essence of our life
It does not wait for past or future
It dashes through life like life itself
The future is the present and the present is the past
The past is end for future's present
The time is entity of life.

Life is time, time is life
Time is hope for future time within
We ought to see time to catch it
We do not see this time but try to work our bidding
To try to catch and see this time we struggle
To catch this time is not our time or place
Our time has not arrived for us
For us to catch the time of life we have to wait
It shines through life of living earth
Time is water in our hands.

N. Madorsky

I never considered that I would start using methods in my practice which I had previously avoided, such as pronouncing in a certain way some elaborately structured phrases, sometimes not having any definite meaning, but still endowed with particular sound quality. Different vibrational frequencies arising during the pronunciation of specific harmonic sound sequences at times perform amazing effects on the chosen life form.

The human body responds differently to sound frequencies with non-specific reactions. For example, the stimulation of immune, nervous and endocrine systems takes place, accompanied by the intensified secretion of corticosteroids and mineralocorticoids and increased resistance activity towards harmful agents.

In all ages and cultures, the idea that certain sound and word combinations produce an influence was widely known and believed. In Russia, they were called "zagovors" or prayers; in Asian countries, they were named "mantras"; in Europe, spells, charms or incantations, sympathies, etc.

Over time, charms both collided and intertwined with religious prayers, while some, because of their real action, became known as prayers and were included in the prayer books. That is how the healing effects of a number of well-known prayers came to be recognized.

Some combinations of sounds and words carry negative information, i.e., energy information of specific polarity and eventually, an undesirable impact. Others perform an entirely opposite action, neutralizing the unfavorable perceivable energy currents in the receiver. The weak informational energy fields created while uttering the coded words fill the healer's own field, permeating all living space, stretching out to the destination, including the target/receiver. Nature maintains balance, and thus carries out one of the main laws of philosophy: unity and struggle of the opposites. Each unfavorable sound combination corresponds in equilibrium to phonetic signals with contrasting qualities. I do not doubt that the reader remembers at least one moment in the past, perhaps normally avoided in his recollections, when a phrase said in a whisper or out loud brought consequences of an unforeseeable nature.

The power of word and thought is boundless in effect. It is capable of revitalizing or mortifying the living substance in front of your eyes. In my childhood the old woman who was my neighbor gave me some daffodil bulbs from those beautifully blooming in her garden each year. I was 12 when they were planted. A year passed, then another; year after year they never flowered. My sister, who lived with my parents, was always tempted to dig them out, but for some reason, she did not venture to do so. Then 25 years after I planted them, right after my parents' deaths, the daffodils suddenly bloomed! I can't imagine with what words or thoughts the bulbs were given, but the result of their actions was astonishing. It is horrifying to think what may have been hidden behind those thoughts, what the thinkers were after and what goal they reached. I sometimes wonder, is it possible? I felt they bloomed to let us know our parents were still around in the spiritual realm. It was simply my parents way of saying "hello".

The foundation of the charm is a strong, manifesting power of the very word. That's why the charm depends upon exact memorization of the word order. It is recommended to never change their text, as their effectiveness is decreased. In my personal practice, I have learned that the main thing in charms is not to touch upon the key words which carry the chief energy load. Since I began to use charms in my practice, I came to the conclusion that there were good reasons that these word combinations were transmitted from generation to generation and were kept secret in families. Only the spiritually mature are worthy to use them. Otherwise, the application of sound effects could lead to unpredictable consequences if they were to get into impure hands. Those who grew up in traditional families learned the power of word and thought. Information about it was passed from generation to generation. The parental school of wisdom was absorbed daily by young minds.

As I mentioned earlier, I became aware of the practice of using charms when my mother could not recover from erysipelas by usual medical treatment. I always remember my parents, who heard our conversations about someone's unseemly behavior, warning us that we must never curse anyone. Those who deserve curses receive them sooner or later, but they must never proceed from us, who must fear the consequences, along with consideration for our descendants.

Once when I was in the maternity ward with my second child, the old nurse on duty had heard a disconcerting reaction from one of the young women. Quite dismayed at what she heard, the nurse told a group of us about an incident. Another mother's child started crying during the night. Roused from her bed, she gave him a slice of bacon, irately adding: "Here you go, stuff your throat with it!" After some time, not hearing any more crying, she decided to check to see if everything was okay. To her terror, she discovered the child choking on the piece of bacon. The woman, almost losing her mind with grief, somehow managed to get the baby to the maternity ward where she had given life to this baby, and pleaded for help. Sobbing, she tried to explain to everybody in the room that she uttered those curses not out of malice. The child could not be saved. This story shocked me and led me to remember a golden rule: think positively, and say aloud only what is positive or, at worst, what means nothing, if you expect blessings in your life.

Subconsciously, the released phrases proceeding from the depths of the soul materialize into reality, sometimes afflicting the message receiver with the effect and, like a boomerang, always returning to the initiator and those surrounding them. It is quite probable that nothing would have resulted without that critical phrase. I do not doubt that in the destiny of each of us, there are similar situations, learning opportunities which we hide in the depths of our memories. Words, pronounced aloud, possess more power if uttered by a person having access to the Universal information field.

Incantations or charms have a special place. They are present historically in every developed ethnic heritage. If one wishes to employ them in practice, it is necessary to decide for what purposes they will be used. If they are used for the sake of good, then it is honorable and noble; but if someone would use them for evil, then he should be prepared to face the undesirable consequences facing those who utter spiteful charms. The negative oral or mental information that is sent out has the ability to reflect off a person endowed with a higher spiritual potential and a pure karma. Like a boomerang, the energy returns to its source. This is very well known to all who engage in underhanded business. When uttering certain charms, they utilize intermediaries, usually in the shape of puppet like images or small animals, that absorb all the reflected information that hasn't reached its destination.

Once, my temperature jumped up to the critical mark and did not subside for several days. At that time, I was perusing a book in which some charms were described. I ran into one very short charm for high fever. I remember thinking that I risked nothing, that the temperature could not climb higher. I conducted my first charm trial on myself because I had never had a personal experience so I read the verse with faith before going to sleep.

For Fever

I shall get up, being the servant of God, (name), with blessing and shall go, crossing myself, towards a blue sea. On the blue sea there lays a rock scalded to whiteness. On this rock there stands the Lord's throne. On this throne there sits Holy Mother. In white hands she holds a white swan, picking and plucking the swan's white feathers: as the white feather jumped away, bounced off, so let the disturbing temperature and the familiar fever jump away, recoil, and bounce off the aching head, the clear eyes, the black liver, the white lung, from hands and feet. You came from the wind – so go back to the wind. If you came from the water – go back to the water. If you came from the woods – go back to the woods. From now till ever.

By the end of the next day when my relatives started wondering and asking about me, my fever was already gone. When one recovers, one soon forgets what had once worried him or her. My fever broke and my temperature was normal in the morning.

Generally, all the charm texts are recited a certain number of times. This one I intuitively uttered three times with expression. From then on, no matter whether the charm designated the number of repetitions or not, it became a ritual for me to pronounce it three times right away. I try to have a burning candle during the recitation, the flame of which amplifies the energy impact of the words.

The pronunciation of the words in a certain way affects our energy-informational fields, reshaping their structure and the connections with the physical body and thus, indirectly acting upon interpersonal relationships. Since then, I have studied much on this subject and have talked with those who practice charms. In most cases, I have run across a shortened version or distorted text. Those who were the originators sometimes intentionally provided changed versions, reducing the effect of the charm. When I need to use a charm, I always conduct a whole investigation with my intuition, which I trust. At the end, I compare the results of the analysis of my inner "I" with the information contained in the Universal information field. Only when the results coincide do I adopt the necessary charm for my usage. In some cases, I have to look through a good number of them until I find the correct one, capable of giving help.

The power of some charms is enormous, and their effects depend in no small degree on who is applying them, and with what feeling, and with how much faith in the expected outcome. While one is uttering a charm with a special intonation, its meaning is revitalized, changing both the surroundings and the ailments. It is often necessary to abide by the conditions accompanying the text, the meaning of which has been lost over the centuries, but still imparts a special power to the words by physical structuring.

One patient had many warts for more than eleven years. It took time for me to convince her to use charms for treatment. She was astonished when the warts disappeared. A friend of our family had a large wart on his foot and had scheduled surgery to remove it when he called me for advice. I dictated one of my charms. Months later he told me about his recovery without surgery. Below are three different charms that can be used. Sometimes the charms need to be repeated until the warts are gone.

The Removal of Warts

• Go to the field, find a dry straw, and pinching the wart, simultaneously recite the spell. Then, bury the straw in the earth in an uninhabited place, so it won't be dug out accidentally.

"As the grass shrivels up and wilts, so let the wart wilt away, melt down."

• Take a raw potato or an apple, cut in two halves, or quarters. Then, with the slices of the potato or apple, rub the warts, simultaneously uttering: "Just as I am wiping my hands with this potato (apple), so let the wart disappear."

Repeat the spell three times. Then, put together the used slices of the potato (apple) and tie snugly with a thread, burying them into the earth in the uninhabited place, so that nobody will ever move them. While burying them, also recite three times: "Just as this potato (apple) will soon decay, so my wart will soon disappear."

• This active way of wart removal was told to me by an acquaintance of mine and had been conveyed to her by her mother. It is preferable to spread either sour cream or butter on the warts and let the dog lick them. The warts will vanish without your noticing, according to the saying, "Just like the dog licked them off with its tongue."

In some cases, one can "charge" water by words of charms and reliance on one's intuition. I allude to the whispered recital of a charm over a container of water, which afterward should be used by my patient internally or externally, according to circumstances. Water possesses the magic universal quality characteristic of all living things – the ability to accumulate biological information which is later transferred to the user. All of us know many tales where miraculous qualities are ascribed to water, such as "living" or "dead." This is factual. All depends on where the coding program is directed – positively or negatively – during the water or juice activation.

A patient's reaction to the sound fluctuations and to the activated water varies quite a bit. Some see or sense with inner vision how the body is entwined with the light or a silver current, while others fall into a state of peace. The water reminds them of some taste experiences from childhood or produces a feeling of warmth circulating through the interior organs.

I recommend keeping the prepared liquid in a glass or glazed pottery dish in a cool, dark place for no more than week. I advise not placing the container holding the liquid into the refrigerator or near any other electrical appliance, due to the undesirable effects of electromagnetic fields generated by house appliances on the embedded bio-information in the water's molecular structure.

While reciting the text, I visualize the flow of the disease or some other aberration in the patient as some living entity incorporated into him which needs to be disciplined. Remember that every negative impact has a more powerful, positive counteraction. Such is the law of nature. It does not like imbalance. One vivid example is when a couple came to me for help. For no known reason, one of the spouses was withering in front of my eyes, while the other was close to sudden death. Dealing with prostate cancer in the husband and the lethal threat to the wife, I discovered the presence of some negative fields around him. They also affected his wife each time she made efforts to save him. After the situation was analyzed, it was uncovered that one of his former employees, upon leaving the job, asked an expert in black magic to destroy his former employer. The fulfillment of the request did not wait to become a reality. Initially, the husband was hospitalized, but upon his release he received a call from the former employee who wanted to know if he was still alive!

Since I could not see any other way to eliminate the consequences of action of dark forces, I offered to conduct a course of treatment for the business which this unfortunate individual owned. I treated the office as a living organism, possessed by the disease, in which my patient spent most of his time. I had to spend some time in searching for the correct charm and also substances that could cleanse the energy space of the building. I learned from this experiment that no matter what expressions are used, and no matter from which religious source the phrases are borrowed, if they are approved by many generations, the positive outcome appears sooner or later as they become incorporated into the energy essence capable of fighting the disease.

The charms were created throughout the ages and were transmitted from teacher to worthy disciple, and usually to the younger, not the older. Those who are not initiated into the business of healing do not have the right to use them. Mobilization and concentration of mental energy is imperative at the moment of reciting the coded verbal information in a state of spiritual elevation. The frequency of sound vibrations during the charm recital adjusts the vibration frequency of the energy field of the living being to its own, until they completely coincide. When resonance occurs, a critical moment in the flow of disease is at its peak.

For more than a month, I had an infection in one of my toes. I tried everything, but nothing worked. For some reason, I never thought about going to the doctor. Maybe I was wary of other problems that could arise if I decided to visit the hospital. As a last resort, I decided to rub plantain (ribwort) on the affected toe. The first time it didn't help. I was truly disappointed. Then I had the idea to speak with the plantain before I cut it. The following recovery was unbelievable. The process was fast. Since then, I always have a conversation with plants before I use them for healing.

While Gathering Medicinal Herbs*

I, who walk in the mountains, forests, and valleys, searching for the medicine to heal people, thank the spirit of this plant. I trust with all my heart that this plant will cure people's diseases. I thank the Highest Spirits of the plants rendering benevolent deeds to those who are in need. Amen.

---

* Prayer of R. Madorsky

The listed charms have been used more than once with positive outcomes and may be beneficial in many situations. I would like to remind you that all of them are only a supplement to the healing procedures of both folk and official medicine. There is a multitude of texts, but the main task of those who utilize them is to choose those which harmonize with their psychoenergetic potential. When the charm is pronounced, the sound vibrations of the words enter the resonance with the energy field fluctuations of both the source (healer) and the receiver (the patient). The charms are often composed intuitively by the healer during a session, and then it becomes important to retain them, to write them down for the next time.

Frequently, we do not distinguish between superstition and folk methods of treatment. This resembles scientific exploration: what is today an unalterable truth may tomorrow become a profound misconception, and vice versa. So-called superstition is often turned into a part of folk medicine. Think about the effect of charms in light of the impact of sound vibrations on the activity of the plant and animal world as confirmed in the sphere of modern scientific research.

Let the prayers and charms bring you and your loved ones deliverance from afflictions or from unhappy circumstances in the hardest time of your life. Good luck to you. And do not be afraid of trying to resonate positively with universal elements. The prayers marked with an asterisk (*) were given to me from above and have been very powerful for many patients and for people who requested them.

While Blessing Candles or Incense

The Spirit of Light! The Spirit of Wisdom!

The breath of which gives and takes the form of each and everything. You, to which the life of the beings is only a changing shadow or vanishing steam! You, who soar above the clouds and gallop on the wings of the wind! The infinite spaces absorb Your exhaling vapors, while inhaling, everything that originated from you returns. The unceasing motion in eternal barrenness, be You blessed for ages to come! We exalt You, we bless You in the transitional kingdom of the created light, shadows, reflections, and images, and always aspire to Your permanent and imperishable luminescence. Let the light of Your wisdom and the warmth of Your love penetrate into our essence; when all that is moving will become crystallized, the shadow will become the body, the spirit of the air will turn into land, and the dream will turn into a thought. We will not be carried away by the tempest and we will hold the winged horses of the morning and direct the currents of the evening winds, so that we can appear before You.

Oh, Spirit of the spirits! Oh, the imperishable breeze of life! Oh, the inhalation of the Creator! Oh, those who inhale and exhale all that exists in the ebb and flow of Your eternal world, which is the ocean of divine movement and truth! Amen.

For a Successful Trip

I am riding from field to field into green meadows into far places, during dawn and sunset. I wash myself with the icy dew, dry off, clothe myself with the clouds, and put on a belt of pure stars. I ride across a pure field, and on the pure field grows the overcoming-grass. Overcoming-grass! It wasn't me who watered you, it wasn't me who gave birth to you, it was the mother Earth who bore you, the straight-hair girls who watered you, and the old women too. The overcoming-grass! Overcome the evil people, so that they would not think spitefully about us, wouldn't ponder anything unclean, push off the sorcerer, the informer.

The overcoming-grass! Help me overcome the high mountains, the low valleys, the blue lakes, the rugged shores, the dark woods, the tree stumps and logs. I walk with you, the overcoming-grass, to the ocean-sea, to the river of Jordan, and in the ocean-sea; in the river of Jordan there lies a whitely-scalded rock – Alatir. How firmly it lies before me, so let the tongue of evil people not turn against me; let their hands not be raised to hurt me, but let them lie firmly, as this whitely-scalded rock Alatir lies. I will hide you, the overcoming-rock, in the zealous heart, for the whole way, for the entire road.

Being Frightened From

I shall get up with blessing, shall go crossing myself
from doors to doors, from gates to gates, to sea, to
the East. Near the sea, on the East, there lies a captive
woman. Above the captive woman there is a cathedral.
In that cathedral there stands the Holy Mother – the Keeper.
I pray and repent – expel all the lessons, alarms from your
Servant, (name), take off from the white face, from the zealous
heart, from the hot blood, from hands, from feet, from
everything. The comely girl strolled in the woods, cut off
the azure flowers with the scissors, poured the full blood
into the Lord's servant, (name).
From now till ever, from earth to heaven.
Amen.

From Painful Periods

"Do not be tormented, soul, do not ache, body, do not whimper, do not prick. Leave the womb's tenement, the woman's ailment. Just as the river flows, washing the rugged shores, the marine vegetation, let the woman's blood flow smoothly from the God's servant, (name)."

Recite this onto water and drink during the first day of a menstrual cycle.

From Migraines

Do not ache, the bone, in the turbulent head. No more pain for the bone in the head, no more strain for the brain. The sick blood will not fill you up, will not shatter the temples of your head, and the God's servant, (name), will not suffer from it. As a beautiful Sunday is, was, and will be, so the health to the turbulent head of the servant, (name), will be preserved forever and ever. Amen.

From Ulcer

Read this onto the water and give it to the sick individual to drink:

"Oh, God eternal, Oh, Heavenly Ruler, a great mercy came upon you, the Creator. Oh, Lord, pray for our sins; we are punished. I recline on my knees with tears. Save us and the God's servant, (name), from this terrible ulcer. Send the God's servant, (name), an angel, a Holy Keeper, with the Holy Virgin and all saints. From now till ever. Amen."

From Misfortune*

I order and command you, o Earthly creatures!
Do not continue any longer the struggle for My servant, (name).
Leave (name) in peace for all the anguish (s)he endured,
that were not removed.
Let all the pains and suffering go away from
My servant, (name), to places unseen and forgotten.
Release, dark forces, My servant, (name),
from terrible torments of hell.
Let all the bloody deeds of My servant, (name), be forgiven.
Turn aside from (name) the covers of night and pain.
Send away from (name) the Angel of bad fortune and fear.
Let the tender fire of life eternal resurrect in the soul of (name).
Let the gentle soul of (name) find its peace and let the happiness
and earthly joy rise in his/her heart.
Let My servant, (name), hear the voice of the Lord our God!
Let these words be fulfilled! Let these words be forever!
Amen!

Prayer for Protection*

Willing to go to the past to re-create my childhood where
I have received tremendous abuse from my enemy
(name), who destroyed my life and the life of my family.
We are working together to fight him for what he did to us.
I don't need to be a victim anymore, and ask God to protect
me from devilish plans which haunted me from my past lives.
I am praying to God to let me know how much I need to be
myself anytime and everywhere.
God, save me from myself for the safety of my descendants.
Help God to protect me from myself and protect my
family from the agonizing energy of our enemies.
God, help me, help me, help me.
So let it be!

From Illness*

Loving earth and sky, asking God to let His light
be with us to help our families live long lives and
willing to go to fight for the freedom of my people.
Help God to heal our souls within our hearts.
Weep God, weep God for our life in our houses.
Weep and weep. Oh, my God!
Help me, God, to be with You during my days.
My time will come to be with You.
Having God in our heart is the only way to fight
our illness in a manner You wanted from me.
I have to go with You to fight my illness. Oh, my God!
Let me do it Your way. Oh, my God!
My illness is not your illness. My soul is not your soul.
My heart is not your heart. But my freedom is your freedom.
So let it be.

Prayer to Achieve Dreams*

I need God for my soul.
Having God in my heart all my life.
Asking God to be with me in all my lives.
Proud to be part of our God every minute.
Having God with my soul, promising God
To have my heart with our God.
My dream, Lord, is to come close to You
In the way You have designed for me.
Telling God all my truth I trust God with all my heart.
Asking God for help to achieve my dream toward my destiny.
I need You, O my Lord! I need You! I need You!
Amen! Amen! Amen!

Prayer for Guidance*

Oh, the Spirit of the Worlds!
Oh, that which gave the life to everything on this earth!
Oh, that which breathed in light into our eyes! We appeal to You
with prayer! Stop, look back, and gaze intently at us – Your
creatures on earth. Relinquish us from our harsh sins. Bring us
deliverance from the deadening curses. Treat us with love and
compassion to our reckless deeds. Open for us the doors of the
future, point to us the righteous way, give us the right knowledge!
Light up our hearts with invigorating fire that is annihilating all
that is useless and terrible!
Oh, our Creator! Oh, our Master! Oh, our Father!
Be merciful to our sufferings and the earthly wishes!
Fill us with health and happiness!
Oh, our Teacher, we thank You for all that was done and is
expected! Let Your existence persist eternally in immeasurable
time and boundless space! Gratitude and reverence from us who
are living and watching You and keeping
Your image in our hearts!
We thank You for all that was accomplished and redeemed!
Peace and tranquillity to our tormented souls!
Happiness and success to our life!
Love and respect to our God!
Amen! Amen! Amen!

Chapter X

THE MIRROR

OF DESTINY

*The God put signs upon people's hands
so that all can know about their actions.*
 —Book of Jacob, Chapter XXVII, poem 7

In Our Hands

*T*he things we try to do in life

The things that make us who we are

Those mentors in our live are helping us to deal with it

There is no time that must be made

There was that time and only that

That makes us who we are in place

We must go to the edge of life

This life of time that has no length

This peace around us in our hands

The time to take that peace away

The time for people to be born

The time for people to be dead

The time that must not come today

The days we cherished in the past

Those are the days that must come now.

N. Madorsky

The art of hand reading, or palmistry, has existed for millennia in all parts of the world. It is trusted because every mark on the hands has been verified by the experience of many generations of readers. Thousands of years before the birth of Christ, the Chinese engraved hands with mysterious lines on the walls of temples and monuments. In India, knowledge about reading palms is not only preserved, but also has developed into the independent science of Hastarik, or the investigation of lines on the palm. The gypsies were one of the castes in India, entertainers of the masses. They left their old fatherland in the beginning of the second millennia, and carried their skill of palmistry on the roads of their migration. In Western civilization, this art has evolved from the time of Ancient Egypt through Greece and the Roman Empire. Europe received palmistry through the mathematician scientist Pythagoras. The earliest European treatise devoted to this topic that has survived to our days was written by Aristotle in 350 B.C. Later, the Roman physician Galen paid his debt to this art by dedicating 250 books to the study of signs of the hand. In the history of palmistry, some widely-known names include the Roman emperor Julius Caesar, Avicenna, and, in the present time, the English scientist and palm-reader Herbert Jenkings (1866-1936).

Such sciences as astrology and palmistry, alchemy and magic have endured, despite the Inquisition, at least 500 years, both in times of prosperity and decay, in favor as well as disrepute from the world of authority. Some scientists now conclude that the lines and the signs on our hands are the surface manifestations of genes that carry the responsibility for the development and formation of the organs of the human body from birth until death.

Another point of view exists – the theory of "subconscious." This aspect of human consciousness is a mystery through which it is possible to explain the presence of a soul in the human being, which knows the past, as well as the present, and possesses knowledge about the future. This soul, photographed and measured on an electronic scale (2-7 grams), transmits information to us through signs and lines of the hand only with one purpose: to warn us and thus, prevent imminent phenomena dealing with the person, or to bring hope and encourage him/her in thoughts and actions.

Why then does the majority of the population of the so-called "civilized world" treat not only palmistry but all other occult sciences with prejudice and wariness? Fear of awareness that destiny is written and possibly pre-determined on the human hands led to the distorted translation of the 37th chapter of Jacob in the Old Testament. The original was: "God put signs upon the people's hands so that all can know about their actions." When translated to languages other than ancient Hebrew, these lines and signs are ascribed to God: "He laid a seal upon the hand of every man, so that all people would know His work" (Book of Jacob 37:7).

During the Middle Ages, the sovereign religions annihilated by sword and fire all the known manuscripts containing knowledge of occultism; they executed those who performed the mysterious metaphysical rituals, as well as those who kept books on these subjects. All of us remember the story of the medieval Inquisition with its trials and fires. This influence suppressed any attempts to explore the occult. Rulers and monarchs changed their attitudes toward the inexplicable powers depending upon the era and public opinion as well as their own desire.

The Mongols, while conquering India and other countries, destroyed all knowledge in occult arts because they were afraid that the vanquished people would use the information to their advantage. History continues and repeats the spirals in its approach to the rediscovered mysteries of being. Knowledge is strength and inspires hope for a change of fate in one or another direction!

In ancient times, one could hear, "This is inscribed upon the palm of my hand." This saying comes to my mind each time I start a conversation with a new patient. Much that has been experienced, witnessed, and predicted can be distinguished from the drawing inscribed by nature on our palms.

The following examples from my practice will help you to understand how it is important to pay attention to oneself and one's hands.

A middle-aged woman, Dagny C., came to me with advanced arthritis in her ankle. During a full diagnosis of her body, which I always conduct no matter what the primary sources of complaint are, I spotted strong functional disorders in the heart. After responding to my advice to visit a specialist to have a cardiogram, Dagny reported that her doctor could not find any problems in her heart and, therefore, there was no need for additional examinations. After her bold statement, I asked for permission to examine her hands. I noted an abrupt stop of the life lines on both hands in the near future and the transformations, reflected on the palms, in heart activity, confirming the accuracy of my words. Without giving much explanation, I offered to work with her heart. The reaction of Dagny's body to the energy correction mechanism convinced her of the accuracy of the diagnosis.

During the course of the therapy session, Dagny pointed out the significant change in depth and length of the life line on her left hand. The next time Dagny came in exalted, telling me that it had become easy for her to breathe and she had stopped feeling difficulties during walking. Her life line was further prolonged. With each session, the condition of her heart and feeling of well-being improved and correlated with visible changes in the lines on her palms.

This case is particularly notable because the patient herself had some knowledge of palmistry and, during her life, had followed her destiny as inscribed on her hand. Fortunately, for Dagny, who perceived the approach of disaster, she had the chance to stop the process and reverse it. Currently, she has not only forgotten about her arthritis, but also her heart is no longer giving any warning signs to me. Her shortness of breath is over, and she has no problem with short jogs.

Our convictions have been forged since childhood: "So what if there are lines. The doctor knows better." The result is a suppression of our deep intuitive impressions regarding our health. This is what it means to listen to one's intuition, the result of knowledge passed on from previous generations. Many people think that fate cannot be influenced in any way. Nothing is permanent; everything has a tendency for change according to our wishes or intentions.

Ted L. was repairing our bathroom and told me in passing that he had a doctor's appointment because a tumor was found on his back. After conducting a distance diagnosis, I located a malignant tumor. After testing his astral fields and energy centers, I confirmed my initial conclusions. During our next conversation, I learned that several years ago he had fallen from a high place and broken his neck. Fortunately, everything went well at that time, without serious consequences.

When I asked him about his dreams, he confided to me that during his youth he had a dream in which he saw his tombstone with the date of his death. This dream astonished him so much that it was preserved in his memory. Ted showed his palms to me. On both palms, the life line stopped at about 40-50 years. It was interesting that Ted knew something about reading the lines of the hand and had already accepted his future. Just as in the previous case, after our conversation an increase in the length and depth of the lines became apparent to his surprise.

Each time I reach the conclusion that the chance of recovery has been granted, the human body – even more likely, the soul – responds instantly, starting to rewrite the given program of health and destiny and changing the shape of the lines on the palms. The soul says to its owner: The decision is in your hands. Do not miss the opportunity bestowed upon you to recover, to prolong your life. Each destiny has its own hand type with unique twists of the lines. What is most peculiar is that, in most cases, the people are familiar with the meanings of the lines.

Another patient, Chris D., had the head line interrupted right at the middle of his palm with an interval of 2.5 cm or 1 inch. At one time in his life, Chris had suffered from strong headaches, requiring medical assistance. Also, in his adolescence, he felt irresistible urges to take part in various risky, life-threatening adventures in which he came close to incurring severe head trauma. This had not happened, only because of constant attention and control from his relatives. After correction of Chris's energy fields, it was discovered that in the place where the head line was interrupted, a thin line was restored, bridging the two halves. With each session, this bridge became more and more pronounced and deep. At the present time, this patient does not suffer from strong headaches and has become more responsible in his activities.

Our thoughts, as well as our completed and unfinished deeds, are all drafted upon our palms. The Book of Moses states: "The hand is the mirror of the individual, in which all of his life is reflected." From time to time, glance at your hands, asking yourself whether everything is all right at the given moment. Our soul, or our subconscious, knows everything ahead of time and wishes to give us assistance. Each day brings new stories and, at times, approaching tragedies which can be prevented.

What can be said about a 27-year-old young man, Dan Z., who is married, a father, and a very nice, simply charming, fellow? There is only one impediment – he is marked by a stamp of early death. Cancer of the rectum was found serendipitously when he brought his uncle to me, who had a stomach ulcer and a pre-cancerous state of the duodenum, for examination. Dan had already an experience with healers, in the course of curing his own stomach ulcer. All the ailments I named were confirmed by him, but he had never confronted cancer of the rectum. The illness did not give any signs; however, his grandmother and cousin had died from cancer.

He took the news about his serious condition very calmly and agreed that the diagnosis was accurate; he already had undergone medical tests. During the subsequent examination of his palms, I recognized alterations on the life lines, both the right and the left palms. On the left one was small breach at 25-30 years, while the right line stopped at an age of 35-40 years!

Many variations of palms, with their coded strings of information, could give us clues to use for our own good! Palm analysis has become part of my routine diagnosis, during which I sometimes enlighten the person and sometimes attempt to guard him against awareness of the inevitable disaster. Some people by nature like to make their own mistakes and learn from them. In other cases, it would be, according to the words of the patient, "… a forceful invasion into untouchable personal territory" to give the information to the patient.

What can the palm lines tell and remind us of? One of the main cautions is the period of time during which we are given a chance and a choice, both to solve conflicts in life situations and in our health. Through the mystical lines of the palm, our soul or our subconscious tries to communicate with us, often years in advance, to warn us about impending danger. The main thing is not to ignore your adviser and instructor – Intuition. Meet the challenge fully armed. In ancient times, it was said: "To be warned in advance is to be armed against a chance."

One gentleman came to me with a problem in his kidneys. Diagnosis showed a presence of cancer cells, which he had suspected. Upon examining his right palm, it became apparent that he actually had been destined to end his life 20 years ago but that strict control over his health and a rigid diet with the necessary amount of minerals and vitamins, together with exercise, extended the length of his life. His hand showed that there had been a chance of death, but he had taken measures at the right time to protect himself, and the left hand reflected it – a long, clear life line with a small interruption at the place indicating the present time, which was eliminated after a number of sessions.

Each time when a new patient consults me, I show him where the sign of warning is located. I ask the patient to memorize it and follow the transformation in the lines of the hand. I'd like to remind you that this is only an additional visual source of knowledge about the state of our physical body. It allows us to be warned in advance about the restoration of our emotional and functional being, soul and body. With each new patient, my collection of palm marks expands. Many, out of gratitude, add to these visual testimonies their own stories about what led them to me and about the process of recovery.

To help you to learn about yourself, I will give you some information which, I believe, can aid you in self-diagnosis. When you are alone, no one can reproach you, saying you are seeking assistance from "quacks." Only your soul and body will be your advisers in the hard search for truth, which can otherwise prevent inevitable trouble. Health and all that accompanies it, including our intellect and our thoughts that proceed from it, are always our first concern. I ask you to consider all the information provided below as an embarkation point toward self-knowledge. It will generally refer to health and all that affects it. It is not a treatise; it's only a beginning.

Healers gifted with paranormal abilities since birth carry distinctive marks on their hands (Fig. 10-1). The appearance of a cluster of short lines on the mount under the pinkie finger, called the sign of care (Fig. 10-1a), identifies the presence of compassion toward people. The mystic cross (Fig. 10-1b) is found in the space formed by the lines of heart and head. It is usually situated under the mount of the second finger, formed by the intersection of one of the lines of the palm with the line of fate. In the cases where the line of fate is not present, the mystic cross emerges by itself. It indicates an inborn inclination towards mysticism, magic and occult sciences.

The presence of the so-called Solomon's ring, a semicircle (Fig. 10-1c), connecting the mounts of the first and second fingers, indicates a prominent natural ability in occult and mystical occupations, and to possess it is the dream of many palm readers. The owner of both above- mentioned signs can reach the heights of occult arts, if he wishes to study them.

The appearance of the so-called four-fingered line (Fig. 10-1d), crossing the middle of the left hand and not resembling any other line, is considered a fortunate sign. The person with such a line is endowed with a vivid magical force, big energy, persistence and strength of will. It is very rarely encountered, and one who may see it is quite fortunate.

The visible sign of defense, easily found on the palms of natural healers, are the squares (Fig. 10-1e), formed by the lines. One such mark is called the sign of protection. It means that the person with that trait will be protected or will evade any type of danger, depending on the line's location on the hand.

Returning to the question of self-preservation and self-protection, I would like to add that only through uninterrupted spiritual nourishment by higher powers is the chosen one granted a reliable system of protection.

There is supporting evidence that our hands are like carriers of information, indirectly pointing to the degree of expression of the power of creation in their owners. The dominant palm, carries information about what has been transmitted from generation to generation, the heritage with which we came into this world; the other one reflects what we have accomplished or what we are in the process of attaining and, sometimes, what may be still lying beyond the limits of our imagination.

- Our past, present, and future are considered interconnected and, for this reason, it is always necessary to look at both palms simultaneously.
- If your right hand is dominant, it reflects what we are creating by our work; but the left hand shows with what we came into this world. For the left-handed, everything is vice-versa.
- Learn to take any information calmly and with open eyes: everything is changing every second right in front of our eyes, and we are capable of changing everything, with a little work upon ourselves.

A map of the hand (Fig. 10-1) gives a well-known representation of the major lines and marks on our palms. Generally, when the lines are studied, their location in regard to small mounts (elevations) as well as their length and depth are considered. Meanwhile, the alterations that the lines undergo on their way, such as intersections, divisions, and breaches, are invaluable sources of information for the investigator.

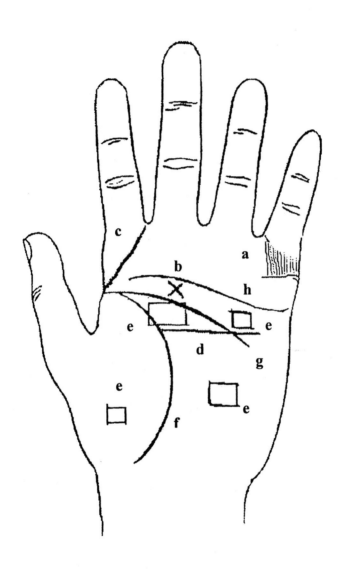

Fig. 10-1

Try to make the process of self-study as scientific as you can. Take copies from the surface of your palm and make comparisons from time to time between your right and your left palm. Try to find differences and identity them in the sketches. A photocopier can make an accurate permanent record. Practice, as a rule, at taking copies of your palms every three months to study them or a guide, and the skill of hand interpretation will come.

Comparing both hands is especially necessary regarding the analysis of health. For example, a person might quite possibly have a badly shaped life line on the dominant hand and a clearly pronounced one on the other. In this case, it is said that, during the first half of his life, the person was in poor health, but with the influence of personal efforts and favorable conditions and a strong constitution has evolved with the corresponding excellent condition of the body.

I will try to concentrate only on those lines of the hand that reflect health, and that warn or guard us from committing errors in regard to helping or knowing ourselves. The interpretation of all cases – and they are large in quantity – is not included in this book. I have not included material dealing with the structure of the hands and fingers or the skin patterns.

Fig. 10-1 shows three major lines, descending from the foundation of the index finger, and called the **life line**, the **head line** and the **heart line**. The first line, encircling the foundation of the thumb, carries the name of the **life line** (Fig. 10-1f). Its position, length, depth, absence of breaches, islands, stars, and other characteristics, determine the general state of health, inborn complexion, and the expected duration of life.

The next one, the **head line** (Fig. 10-1g), starts between the thumb and the index finger. In most cases, its origin merges with the life line, and then diverges and crosses the palm. Its pattern indicates the state of the human mind, power of concentration, and capacity toward self-control. Its significance is realized when the role of reasoning is recognized in the normal body functions. It does not matter how physically fit the body is; if the brain is not in a healthy state, the body cannot work in a normal pattern. The brain is the force which allows us to create the map of our life. Our motives – the driving characteristics of each living thing are the key to the future of its possessor. The brain is the center from which the distribution of vital strength proceeds and where one can locate diseases generally linked with the nervous system.

The third one, the **heart line** (Fig. 10-1h), passes under the mounts and the foundations of the fingers. It reflects the heart's performance – healthy or defective, good or evil.

The **life line** passes through the mount under the thumb and, in many cases, terminates near the foundation of the hand. The life line reflects the health of its owner during various periods of life, his general physical strength, and, in which periods of life he relies more upon sources of nervous strength or muscular energy. It also pinpoints the possibility of the end of a life and, furthermore, shows its premise. As a general rule, the more expressed and the longer the line is, the stronger is the individual's health, and vice versa, the shorter the life line, the shorter the life itself.

However, experience has shown that although in most cases it parallels reality, there are still variations in interpreting the meaning of this line. If its designation is not compared to the other lines of the head, heart, reason and health, there could be mistakes in analyzing the life line.

The examination of both palms is one of the main components of the reading procedure of the life line, since one of the hands can secure the vital capacity of the other, and vice versa. In all palms where a good, long life line is visible, be assured that the inherited health will last long. But in the opposite case, danger is waiting for the person. It is in one's power to take all measures of caution regarding one's own life.

One who is endowed with a thin life line is of a more delicate, nervous nature, than the one having a deep line, and is more prone to fear in fighting with inevitable sickness. A wide line composed of small pieces (Fig. 10-2a) indicates the absence of endurance, and people who have the pattern are very susceptible to all kinds of disorders since they have weak constitutions, inadequacy in natural energy, and do not apply the efforts desired. A line similar to a ladder has the same meaning (Fig. 10-2b).

A life line (Fig. 10-2c) composed of links in the shape of a chain is a clear manifestation of decreased endurance and

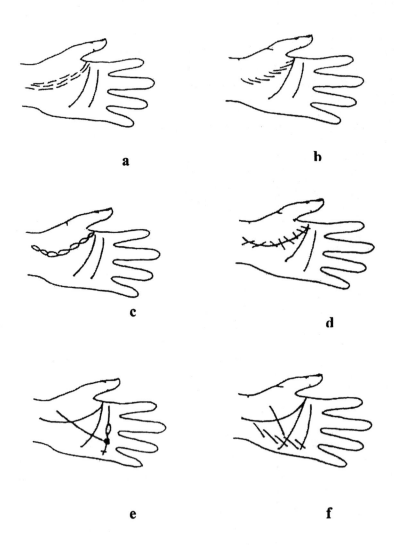

a

b

c

d

e

f

Fig. 10-2

tenderness, and its owner is inevitably endowed with suffering from numerous, redundant, and annoying illnesses.

Conspicuous lines crossing the life line signify experienced or expected diseases (Fig. 10-2d). Their locations can serve as markers of past as well as forthcoming diseases. If these lines are thin, then there is no serious illness. But the level of discomfort and number of occurrences will still equal the number of lines intersecting the life line.

If one of the intersecting lines situated on the life line is directed towards a dot, islet or the breach in the heart line underneath the middle finger, its owner suffers from a heart disorder (Fig. 10-2e). The effects of this sickness can be spotted either on the life line or on the heart line.

An intersecting line proceeding in the direction towards the ladder-like health line (Fig. 10-2f) reveals an onset of stomach problems. If the intersecting line is directed towards the wavelike health line, then hepatitis and other liver disorders are indicated (Fig. 10-3a). If this line is directed toward the net (Fig. 10-3b), located below the mount under the fourth finger, then one has troubles dealing with either blood composition or throat-bronchial problems.

An appearance of islets on the life line (Fig. 10-3c) in the form of branches, closing in on the line itself, points to periods of fragility in health; while their end shows the completion of this period. The size and number of islets tell whether the illness is one-time only or its owner can expect a series of complications, whether there will be a serious long-lasting ailment or a short-term disruption, or if there is a possibility of a chronic sickness. A combination of islets with such marks as dots, breaches, stars, or cross-bars on the life line as well as the lines of the heart, head, and health, give additional information about the nature of diseases and their duration.

Such signs as nets, crosses, cross-bars and all other threatening signals located on certain mounts and lines of the palm help to establish the cause of the organism's malfunction and to prepare for the impending battle. For example, if the islets show up on the heart line (Fig. 10-3d), the general heart weakness will promote the fragility of the body, reflected by the islet on the heart line.

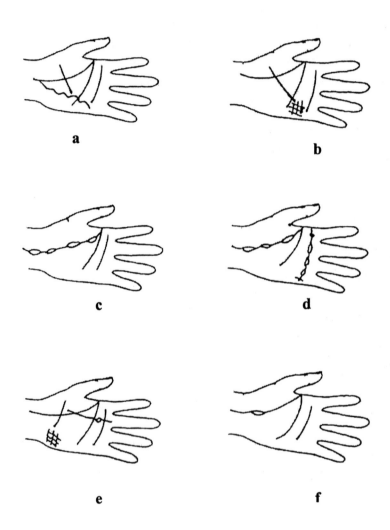

a

b

c

d

e

f

Fig. 10-3

If the line of intersection is toward the middle of the mount of the Moon (Fig. 10-3e), especially to the net that is on it, and in addition, there is possibly another line with an islet targeted towards the second finger, then arthritis and rheumatism are undoubtedly present.

If the intersecting line is going towards the net, a cross-bar, or a cross on the lower part of the mount of the Moon, troubles with kidneys, urinary bladder or gynecological problems will appear. However, if the life line is good-looking with the above mentioned signs, then all the types of problems are natural for its owner and the line points to a strong physical body, and the owner is endowed with the ability to overcome and banish the ailment.

Diseases are read on the life line, but financial success and economic welfare are decoded on the lines advancing toward the third and fourth fingers. Although poor condition of the health can be reflected on that line as well.

The presence of an islet on the life line for women between the ages of 42 to 46 is a common phenomenon (Fig.10-3f). It reflects the age hormonal transformations begin and the length of this period. The impact of these changes upon the person is determined by the quality of the line after the island. If you have noticed such events before the appointed moment of their manifestation, take some measures of precaution.

It makes no sense to list all fluctuations in health foretold by the signs on our palms. Those who are interested in getting more detailed information on palmistry should read more on that specific subject. My purpose is to help you develop curiosity searching for self-knowledge so that possible disaster can be eliminated or its speed and magnitude reduced by a timely visit to a doctor or energy healer using your palms natural blueprint, or even allow time for healing yourself in this eternally unceasing kaleidoscope of life.

The diseases of youth are marked in the beginning of the life line, the diseases of middle age in the middle, and the diseases of old age are reflected at the end.

The life line can be divided into nine parts, each of which represents ten years of one's life, therefore the timing of each event can be determined with some degree of precision. A line composed of two parts points to a fatal disease or sudden death. If, in the beginning, it branches off, forming a fork, that attests to good health. A long but very thin life line exposes the nervousness of the person, while its abrupt disappearance forecasts a near paralysis. Its gradual waning is the sign of a concealed, consuming and long illness, consistently advancing its owner towards death.

If a conspicuous branch diverges from the life line to the mount of the first finger, it is the sign of a dangerous sickness which came as the result of lustfulness. In any case, it is necessary to verify the possible presence of the so-called second life line, passing along the first one or inside it, which protects the outer life with additional endurance. One who possesses such a line escapes death in the most dangerous situations. I have had patients who were endowed with it since birth, but in some cases it stopped, and problems started to emerge.

My opinion, arising from my long-term practice, is that all unfavorable lines are warnings from nature, which is concerned about you, and you have to take precautions, starting by changing your way of life and ending with vigilance. Persistence and a wish for a life of full potential leads to the emergence of connecting lines in the place of a breach, which I have observed many times. It is interesting to observe the birth of such bridge directions and to rejoice with their creators.

Those who are mentally retarded or mentally exhausted, have their life line ending in a fork. A long trip or vacation is recommended to restore the mental potential. Actually, in such cases, many famous writers, artists, and scientists have cured themselves.

The head line. The head line has the same natural location on the palm of the hand as the facial features, i.e., any abnormality in its position marks deviations in mental inclinations. The origin of the head line is between the thumb and index finger, and in most cases, is connected to the life line at its beginning, but then separates from it, crossing the palm. If the head line is very short, then it means either death at an early age, or the loss of reason. If it ascends towards the foundation of the second finger (Fig.10-4a), then one of these tragic events will happen without any doubt, with the same meaning as the appearance of a star, a cross, or a dot at the end of the line (Fig. 10-4a). If the end of the head line has a forked line, then paralysis is near, which won't be a surprise (Fig. 10-4b).

Some of the important marks on the head line are the islands (Fig. 10-4c). They record full or partial shock to mental powers, as long as this islet lasts. The nature of the shock is determined by the location of the island on the line, and it is necessary to establish its time, comparing the information with the readings from the life and health lines. If this islet is present on a child's hand, it is necessary to protect his or her brain from overexertion until it becomes less apparent or vanishes entirely from the head line.

The presence of a chain-shaped head line (Fig. 10-4d) points to a weakness of the brain, which cannot be given any mental exertion or responsibility, as it can lead to madness. When this chain is completed or initiated, a process of recovery or the weakening of mental activity begins. If the head line consists of many small lines instead of one, then it is necessary to note, the probability of getting a mental paralysis. In such cases, a quiet, unhurried life without special stresses is recommended (Fig. 10-4d).

The color of the head line also plays a part during palm reading. White points to an insufficient blood supply to the brain due to poor heart performance, the result of which can be its failure at any moment. A blue tint shows overexertion in the blood circulation in the brain.

Pink intensifies productivity of the brain and reduces some of its deficiencies. Red intensifies the work of the brain, and its deficiencies are not accentuated; but if the chain-like line is present, the actions of its owner can be manifested with an aggressive aim.

The presence of red spots and the appearance of dots or teeth during pressing on the head line indicates a possibility of accidents relating to the head. Dots on the head line are the markings of an acute brain disease which is more or less intense, depending upon their size and color. If the dots are small and white or pink, it signifies illness, but not a fatal one. When the

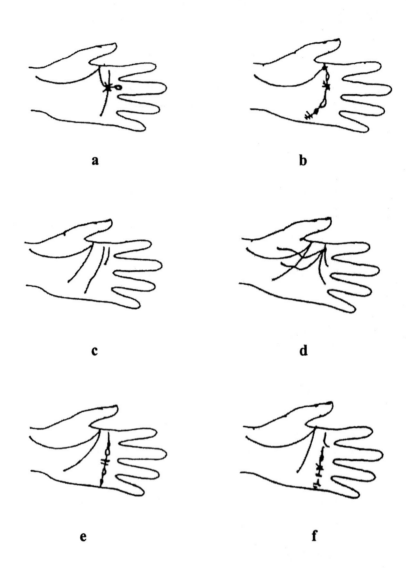

a

b

c

d

e

f

Fig. 10-4

dots are big, red, or burgundy, the brain disorders demand the most meticulous care for oneself at the age when they appeared, while the character of a line following after the dot will illustrate what consequence this illness will have on the head. It will mainly happen if its owner was born between March 21st and April 27th.

The presence of a square, triangle, or a circle on the head line is the sign of protection and circles intensify the mental power. Stars represent the opposite.

A breach in the head line (Fig. 10-4e) generally presupposes an incident after which the head would be damaged or the possible onset of madness. If the fate line merges with one of the breaches on the head line, this indicates an indirect head trauma with lethal outcome. In this case, there is no need for a short life line. If the head line stops opposite the mount of the second finger (middle finger), this is a sad forecast of death resulting from stroke.

A head line interrupted at the end presages a wound of the throat or head, but it could even be madness. A head line ending in a star, chain, deep dot, cross or breaks in the area of the plane of Moon indicates the psychological instability of its owner (Fig. 10-4f).

In a case where the head line connects with the heart line, there is a chance of death during youth. The same result occurs when it is ascending upwards to the foundation of the second finger and there is a star at the intersection of these lines (Fig. 10-5a).

A cross in the middle of the head line suggests about the possibility of a complicated illness or the effect of dangerous trauma. The presence of stars is always a sign of danger. If the cross is located at the end of a short head line, it is interpreted as the cessation of mental activity leading towards death.

If there are intersections at the beginning of the line, this indicates the presence of leg diseases related to falling from a staircase or ladder. If it is intersected by many sidelines, it testifies to an immoral life and venereal diseases.

If the head line is positioned close to the heart line, it presupposes a weak heart, and those who are endowed with this combination usually suffer from heartaches, more frequent heartbeats, fits and swoons. An overly thin head line illustrates frequent headaches, diseases of the liver, and poor digestion.

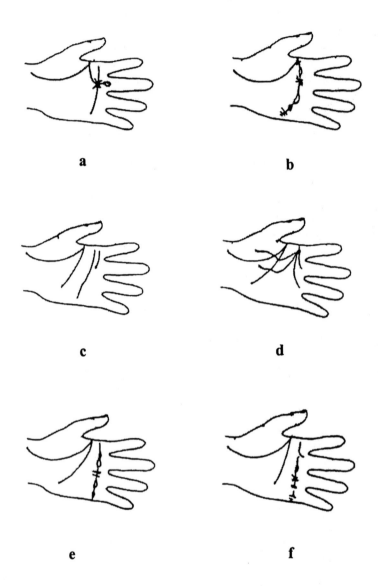

a   b

c   d

e   f

Fig. 10-5

If there is a star at the end of the line, then it points to a near madness or sudden death, and a circle above the head line (under the ring finger) foretells blindness.

A presence of dots, islets, crosses, and stars on the thin head line (Fig. 10-5b) shows dangers for mental activity, which must not pass unnoticed, for measures of precaution must be immediately employed and targeted to the particular age of onset.

The magnitude of the intersections of the head line and their location points to dangerous moments. When they are small and frequent, this indicates headaches, but if they are deep and located on the thin head line, it indicates head fever, nervous exhaustion, or paralysis.

All the listed defects of the head line show that the psychological activity of the person is not always constant and regular but is rather strong. Those formations represent the functions of the brain in a certain period of life. They forecast the time of the onset of health problems, alternating periods of weakness and illness, with consequent interference with the mental powers of the individual which affect his or her destiny. The thickness of the line is a marker of the quality of psychic activity of the brain. Its changes manifest when the person was either mentally strong or weak, when the psychological abilities became concentrated and pressure on the brain increased.

If the head line is thin in the beginning, and becomes deep this points to moments of intensified pressure upon brain activity. In this case, it is a very dangerous line. If it is also marked with a star, cross, or dots, then paralysis, epilepsy or madness are quite feasible. In those cases, only reinforced care about one's health, abundance of sleep, and absence of agitation can be the only advice to its owner!

In each case, it is very important to look at both hands. Only in such cases can a correct forecast be established that leads to recovery. The head line reflects the activity of the brain, demanding considerable attention.

The heart line. The heart line bears its name because it impartially reflects the state and activity of this organ. This line is very important since it deals with the organ which pumps and controls the quality and amount of blood flow, which affects our health and temper.

The heart line passes at the base of the mounts located at the foundation of the fingers. The absence of this line sometimes presages an inevitable disaster. The head line is always present because it controls and maintains all other lines.

A pink tint of the line indicates good health and good will of its owner, while contrary qualities are characteristic of a line with a white tint. A yellow heart line doubles the qualities of a white one. A blue heart line signifies an overload and delayed activity of this organ.

The length of the line indicates the qualitative functions of the heart (Fig. 10-5c). The shorter it is, the greater the probability that the person will have serious difficulties at the age when it stops, even when all the other lines have a normal length.

An abrupt breach in the heart line means that either the heart will stop beating or the heart is small. A heart line passing through the whole palm indicates the presence of a generous heart that will benefit the person who possesses it. In short, the longer the heart line is, the more favorable it is for the future (Fig. 10-5c).

In cases where the heart line turns away from its course and descends downward intersecting head line, serious trauma or damage will be suffered during the time where this event is marked on the head line. This includes mental imbalance, serious brain disorder, blindness, heart problems, paralysis, or death. Such manifestation cannot take place without a natural calamity or a catastrophe. This can be an electric short circuit, explosion, a burn – all relating to the brain (Fig. 10-5d). In any case, it must be perceived as a very serious warning to our omniscient soul. Also, if the point of intersection is deep and red, it is a dangerous sign of approaching disaster.

The most unpleasant phenomenon is when the heart line intersects both the head line and the life line (Fig. 10-5d). In this case, you must know that harm to one's head will take place and, when the life line is short, death can be expected.

If the heart line begins where the life line and head line start and is repeated on both palms, this presages a sudden death. But if this sign is apparent only on one hand, this presages lung and heart diseases. Sometimes, the heart line, starting under the first finger, terminates underneath the second or third one (Fig. 10-5d), attesting to the possibility of serious heart and other illnesses and even short life. An exception is when it stops underneath the third finger – it is the influence of financial complications.

The most favorable heart line is uninterrupted, deep and smooth, without any islands or other defects, with healthy tint and normal length. If the heart line manifests chain formations through its course or in certain places, the general interpretation is a cardiac deficiency and a bad influence of the heart upon the vital activity of its owner in certain periods of his life (Fig.10-5e). Numerous intersections of the heart line attest to constant irritation of the heart (Fig. 10-5e).

In each case, it is mandatory to consider the heart line and the life line together. More serious attention must be devoted to transformations in the heart line if they appear underneath the mount of the third finger, occurring at ages of 40-43. The presence and size of islets on the heart line are signs of a physical problem and its size in the heart activity (Fig. 10-5e). Dots on the lines of the hand are the sign of deviations in health. But if they are on the heart line, something is wrong with the heart – their magnitude demonstrates the seriousness of the situation (Fig. 10-5e).

If there is a chain-like line after a breach on the heart line (Fig. 10-5f), this signifies that the working of the heart will never be fully restored. And when a clearly visible star is present on a spot, its owner will either unexpectedly die at that certain age or will have a very serious bout of heart problems (Fig. 10-5f). When one end of the ruptured heart line has a transverse line running through it, this is, in most cases, a sign of sudden death due to heart failure. The presence of such a sign on both ends is a high probability of death (Fig. 10-5f).

In any case, when dangerous signs are discovered, it is necessary to search for restorative clues (Fig. 10-6a). When the meanings of the lines are deciphered, one must not hurry with conclusions and hasten to inform the person about the unpleasant news. It is always necessary to consider any line on the palm in connection with the others on both palms. Indeed, one hand can turn the situation around 180 degrees. The presence of only one

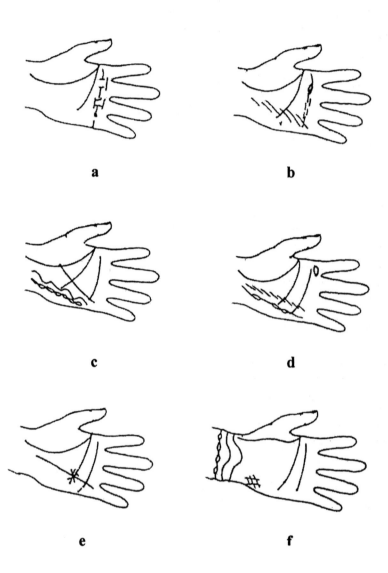

a

b

c

d

e

f

Fig. 10-6

unfavorable sign is insufficient to determine the impending trouble, for other favorable signs can modify or completely compensate for the primary cause. My long-term healing experience has demonstrated more than once that, knowing the cause can change the effect. The main thing is to recognize the approach of danger in time. To be armed in advance with knowledge means to be a winner. It makes no sense in this book to try to describe precisely every small detail of the lines dealing with the health of the person. My task is to provide you with necessary, basic knowledge about our maps of health located on our hands, so that you, can devote a few minutes to study yourself. In preparing for the battle for one's health, one must use various methods, beginning with changing one's way of life, nutrition and diet, physical and sexual activity, and finishing with the search for a good doctor and energy healer. Without a doubt, anything and everything is prone to change if one can recognize an approaching disaster in a timely manner. Even if it cannot be avoided completely, at least one can gain some time from fate and alleviate the power of a shock.

The health line. I will give you a little bit more information about another important line. This line bears various names: the line of health, liver, mercury or hepaticas. Generally, the health line must start on the mount of Moon and go towards the mount of the fourth finger.

This line is valuable because it is an indicator of the digestive tract, especially the liver, and also informs us about the presence of various diseases which arise because of dysfunctions in the digestive system. Doctors joke: nothing keeps our brain out of difficulties like good digestion and a healthy liver!

When defects on the head line are considered, the health line is of remarkable assistance, for it is generally known that the stomach and the liver affect the physical state of the brain. Malfunctions in heart activity also frequently arise because of disturbances in digestion (Fig.10-6b). In such cases, the process of healing must be directed towards recuperation of the digestive system, and the heart ailments will disappear by themselves.

Poor health can destroy a career that is seemingly successful, and this can be explored by the lines of health in relation to the lines of destiny and success. Not everyone has the health line – I would even say half of mankind – while the rest rarely have it well expressed. There is only one explanation for this finding – only a few are endowed with good health. If we had the right to choose, then it is better not to have the line altogether. This is said because we would then be creators of our own health and wouldn't live according to directions from above.

One of the unpleasant indicators is when the health line ascends from the life line (Fig. 10-6c). However, thin lines connecting the life line with the health line may not negatively influence the state of health.

A deep and vivid health line arising from the foundation of the palm towards the mount underneath the fourth finger attests to a good digestive system, healthy liver, vital endurance, purity of reason, excellent memory, and vice versa if it is not deep and vivid.

If dots, islets, cross-bars or other unfavorable signs interrupt the health line or are placed near its end, it is more likely that this person will not recover from illness in the digestive systems.

When the life line has defects, is thin, or is in the shape of a chain, and the health line is deep and pronounced, then this action will overrule the discrepancies in the life line.

The hand which has strong lines of life, heart, and head, with a deep health line foretells that the owner of this palm will never know the meaning of the word "illness."

A chain-like health line (Fig. 10-6c) testifies to the presence of disease-like conditions in the liver or stomach. Its owner is disposed towards inflammation of bile ducts, cirrhosis, and formation of gallstones and to a variety of other diseases dealing with the gastrointestinal tract, mostly serious, and sometimes with sad consequences.

The health line is undesirable since its owner will suffer from subsequent effects: mental apathy and depression. With his or her pessimism, nervousness, and biliousness she or he will try to crush not only oneself, but also one's loved ones, whether one wants to or not.

A wavelike health line (Fig.10-6c) reflects chronic conditions of the bile. Most likely there will be attacks of bile, malaria and various diseases of the liver, frequently ending with its amplification and yellow fever.

A health line resembling a ladder (Fig. 10-6d), points to such serious stomach disorders as dyspepsia, gastritis, and ulcers. The presence of an islet on the health line does not always indicate gastrointestinal problems, but it requests some attention to a particular fragility of health at a specific moment of time. For example, if the life line is composed of a series of islets, this probably attests to the sensitivity of the throat and lungs (Fig. 10-6d). If in addition to that, an islet on the mount underneath the first finger is spotted (Fig.10-6d), efforts will be required to avoid bronchitis, pneumonia, tuberculosis, and other diseases dealing with the throat, the bronchi and the lungs.

If a star is positioned on the health line in the point of intersection with the head line on a woman's hand, then there is a question of a serious gynecological illness (Fig. 10-6e). If this star is located at the meeting point of the health line and the head line, it is a warning about possible complications during pregnancy or about sterility. On a man's hand, the palm with a defective health line and the sign of a star is a serious danger threatening the brain, including possible madness. If the area of the lower portion of the mount of Moon on a woman's hand is covered with a net and demarcations (Fig. 10-6f), then her body is very weak. These women should expect difficulties during pregnancy, while if the life line passes too closely to the thumb finger and circumscribes the mount of Venus, barrenness will probably result.

The same meaning is implied by the rosette line, which is the closest to the palm (Fig. 10-6f) and has the shape of an arch. In antiquity, the appearance of this line was a barrier for a woman to marry due to danger to her life during childbirth. If the second rosette line (Fig. 10-6f) is curved like the first, more serious dangers are on the way for this woman during childbirth, and restoration of health will be prolonged. If the third rosette line is in the shape of a series of small islets (Fig. 10-6f), or if it reaches the middle of the wrist, the chance of fragility of internal organs is more intensified.

The health line must always be viewed as secondary in importance to the lines of life, head, heart, and fate, to the structure and form of the nails with their present defects, and also to the character of the person examined.

It is impossible to embrace all of the nuances which are portrayed by the lines of our palms in this chapter. The purpose of this brief excursion into the world of palmistry is to acquaint you with one of the methods of self-study and self-help, and to explain an additional diagnostic tool which I use in my practice to control my own health as well as the health of my patients.

Chapter XI

A VISION
FOR
EVERYONE

*If gods love people, they will certainly
reveal to them their intentions in a dream.*
—Cicero

*Our dreams are a second life. I have never
been able to penetrate without a shudder
those ivory or horned gates which separate
us from the invisible world.*
—Gerard De Nerval

Making Dreams

*T*he fluency of life is flowing in our midst

The rivers of our hopes try to get free
The hopes that we will hold forever
The borders that protect us in our needs
To hold all hopes we try to keep, be strong when down.
To keep that only hope we have and time is passing by
We try holding on to our dreams for just another minute
The dreams of wealth we have in store
The dreams of fame we build in life
The time is short there is no time to wait
To make our dreams come out and play
To play among the doubters of our life
Those that were doubting that we will make it
To make it to our finish line in time
To make that dream that we are living in our hopes
They are doubters that we hate
We hate with passion in our strength
The strength is coming from inside
To crush those doubters that we hate
There is the way we can emerge
Emerge with life that is our dream.

N. Madorsky

In the Old Testament, we learn that "When there are prophets among you, I the Lord make myself known to them in visions; I speak to them in dreams".

I did not attribute much significance to dreams for a long time, despite the fact that my mother treated them as trustworthy. She learned the art of deciphering dreams in her childhood. Almost every morning, we told her about our dreams. The meanings of positive ones she eagerly deciphered, while the ones that were unfavorable were simply avoided. This became a morning ritual accompanying our preparations for school.

My personal attitude towards dreams changed many years later, after meeting a boy of ten or eleven years of age. He was under treatment in the clinic for infectious diseases for a second time, but with another problem. His story gave me a basis to consider dreams in a new light.

Before he was taken to the medical facility for the first time, he had a dream in which a snake, coiled under a log, bit him. In a week, he was in the clinic for infections. In a few weeks, after he was released from the hospital, he again experienced a similar dream with the snake. Nobody believed him or paid any attention at that moment. But in another week, he again found himself in the same hospital, but with another rare disease. All of the medical personnel were astonished by this case, since it was not possible to get this disease in the hospital, not to mention at home or school.

From then on, I started to analyze dreams. The majority of dreams do not leave a trace in memory, but some of them are not forgotten despite long time periods that elapse. Some of them are to warn, others to encourage; yet still others allow us to look into the future, sometimes years before they come to be true in life. My aroused interest in the dreaming process inspired me to seek literature devoted to investigating this millennial "mystery of mysteries" of our being.

Historically, individuals who were capable of decoding dreams were honored in all civilizations and were at the service of pharaohs and monarchs, oracles and priests, visionaries and researchers. How many have dealt with our nightly "journeys?" Plato and Socrates, Freud and Jung, Adler and Fromm, Pavlov and Heidegger, as well as many other world renowned scientists, have left their mark in this science, with discussions that never cease, while actual results from dreams, enter our daily lives.

According to Freud's ideas, "The Apparent Dream," i.e., our perception of the dream is a facade which, in the beginning, does not allow us to guess about the inside of the house. On the contrary, the facade elaborately conceals it by so-called censorship of the dream.

However, in keeping with certain technical rules, if we force the one who saw the dream to speak about the details of it, we soon discover that his fantasies possess a certain direction and are concentrated on a particular content and have a personal significance. The dream expresses a meaning which we originally did not expect to find behind it, but which, as can be shown by means of thorough comparative analysis, is in direct, intricate, and meticulous connection with the facade of the dream....

A dream often has to do with details that are seemingly absurd, which explains why it produces such a strange impression, so that we can be amazed by it, at best. Therefore, we always have to overcome a familiar resistance before we seriously start to ponder how we can unravel its complicated and twisted web.

When at last we enter into the actual meaning of the dream, we find ourselves in the center of the secret world of the dreamer. Surprisingly, we can see that the dream, seemingly senseless, has a very deep meaning and tells only about important and serious things. Such knowledge gives us a somewhat greater respect towards so-called superstition, providing significance to the dreams which the rationalistic mental disposition of our time does not respect.

As Freud said, the analysis of dreams is "via regia" or the "royal road" to the subconscious. The analysis of dreams leads to the deepest secrets of the personality, making it an invaluable instrument in the hands of the physician or the instructor of the soul. Freud's conclusions regarding dreams along with all the other widely-known theories, have not yet been given a final verdict.

The time of sleep can be considered as the time of connection of our brain microprocessor to the Universal Processor or the Supermind, during which our subconscious mind receives very important messages dealing with both our personal problems and health, as well as global dilemmas. This Network does not have abrupt interruptions. The dreams come in turns, and their duration fluctuates between seconds and 5-6 minutes. Only the most crucial ones are preserved in our memory. This period of time is identical to Internet transmission, but only on the psychological, subconscious level.

Many of the greatest discoveries were made in dreams. One example is when the psychologist Otto Loewe saw in his dream the technique of an experiment which could have verified the accuracy of his theory of nerve impulses. The experiment reproduced according to
his dream confirmed the correctness of his theory consequently, bringing him the award of the Nobel Prize. All of us remember the classic example of the modern periodic table of elements by Mendeleev – in his dream, the scattered cards with the names of chemical elements were put in their proper order, giving birth to the current version of the table.

Once, working with a patient, I mentioned the significance of sleep in our lives and its relationship to the psychological state of the individual. To my surprise, he expressed a somewhat different point of view. I hope that the originality of his ideas will attract your attention:

"So, why are dreams not recalled sometimes? They are almost never recalled. We vividly see the events and pictures in the dream and acutely perceive all the images and even the tactile impressions. Then, in the morning, we are at a loss; we cannot recollect the details of the dream. This is because thoughts – the thinking in the dream and thinking in the earth world – have entirely different vibrations, other chemistries, and distinct levels of energies. In the earth configuration, all our mind processes occur with the help of chemical reactions. The thinking process of the brain is equivalent to specific chemical bonds and must be transmitted through the earth configuration. When a human being enters a new level of world awareness and his current knowledge is insufficient for explaining the ascertained principles, he is less capable of thinking chemically. To reach higher concepts is impossible without a transition to a different energy level of thinking, which does not correspond with the earth's level of thinking. This is what lies at the foundation of the thought dispersion in people. Training is necessary to eliminate the disconnectedness of thoughts, words and sentences."

"Some psychological disorders can be aberrations in the multi-layered spirit, which in its earthly expression cannot completely fit into its thin earth shell. If the spirit is multi-layered, then the imperfections of an earthly life and the absence of harmony of the physical body with the spirit produces deviations, manifested in some form of odd behavior which cannot be raised to normal parameters. A psychologically balanced individual is the insufficiently developed spirit."

We are still resistant to face the truth regarding our own health and the health of our relatives. Much information dealing with the contents of dreams and their interpretation has been accumulated by humanity. Differing in attributes, appearing in dreams, depending on the cultural or historical environment, they are united by something similar – the commonality of unfolding actions. As was written 2,000 ago by the Roman consul and writer Cicero (106-43 BC), "Nothing can be so silly, so impossible, or so unnatural, that it cannot happen in a dream."

Dreams can foretell the presence of perfect health, as well as the generation or the presence of a disease. Dreams that come in the beginning of sleep usually do not leave a trace in the memory and, therefore, do not have consequences. But the dreams that come in the morning have the ability of being registered in our memory and are mainly actualized.

The analysis of multitudes of dreams allowed me to group them according to reactions. The reactions can amount to both positive as well as negative consequences. The positive results of the dreams or actions we take for granted, but we do not evaluate dreams with negative results. With timely response to the received warning in a dream, much can be evaded or, at least, some measures can be taken to decrease the impact of imminent danger in health.

Despite my desire, it is impossible to list all dreams that pertain to our health and the length of our existence in this world in this book, and it is not my present task. Below, you will find the dreams that can signal approaching danger or give a hint about a needed medical examination by an attending physician.

Abortion. For a woman, it is a warning regarding her health.

Agate. Agates or other semiprecious gemstones point to sadness, disease, or reversals in business.

Adieu. Parting with someone in the dream is the signal of an unhealthy state of the body.

Air. To dream of fresh and pure air is a good sign. To see air polluted and cloudy means illness and sadness.

Ailments. Getting ailments in the dream means medical problems. To have ailments means a careless attitude to one's pleasures.

Amazement. For the sick person, it means recovery.

Amber. Amber in a dream forecasts tears, but to eat it signals yellow fever.

Anemia. Your health will be good.

Amiability. A dream about friendliness means insanity.

Animals. To see or hear wild animals is generally a good dream. A bite from one of them warns to be on the alert from a false friend. If they talk to you, it usually means illness and suffering.

Anvil. To hear the sound of an anvil in a dream is a good sign. It means good health, industrious labor, and joy.

Anxiety. To worry in a dream is the sign of personal trouble. A consultation with the doctor or other qualified specialist is necessary.

Appetite. To satisfy one's appetite in sleep with a particularly favorite food means that you will soon lose your healthy appearance and weight, causing your friends to worry.

Apple. To eat ripe and sweet apples in a dream means health, joy and pleasure.

Apricots. To see or to eat an apricot in its ripening season in a dream means good health and pleasure; but if it's not their season, it signifies a chain of troubles.

Asthma. For those who do not have it, it is a signal dealing with an inflamemation of the lungs, however, with subsequent recovery.

Bacon. Rancid bacon is advice to visit a doctor.

Baldness. A presence of baldness on one's head points to the necessity of a medical exam. There is a chance of a heart problem.

Ballet. To watch a ballet performance in the theater points to spasm of gout or rheumatism, sometimes serious.

Barley Field. To walk across the field or to mow in the wrong season is the sign of imminent trouble, including illness, wrong choice of a spouse, loss of relatives or a meeting with the doctor. It may take you and your friends months or years to solve the problem.

Bathing. To bathe in pure water in a dream means health and success in initiatives.

To bathe in turbid waters forecasts death of a friend or relative.

Beard. For a child to see that he has a beard is the forerunner of death.

Berries. Berries in a dream predict tears, but to eat them raw foretells illness. To eat dried or sweetened berries means profit.

Biography. Reading a biography signals a serious illness of a family member.

Biscuits. The use of biscuits in food means an upset stomach and the necessity to keep a strict diet to prevent further problems.

Blood Flow. A dream of one's own flowing blood foretells headache, migraine or consumption. To spit out one's blood means illness. It does not matter who had the blood discharge in the dream. Any form of it tells you that your physical or psychological, and possibly both states are in critical conditions. Try to relax more.

Bones. Fish bones point to the need for a medical exam; human bones, a coming of inheritance.

Bottle. An empty bottle signifies illness.

Breast. One's own breast in a dream foretells health and happiness. A full and firm breast means long life and welfare in old age.

Bullet. A wound by a bullet in a dream foretells a sneaking physical danger, or danger caused by unfaithful friends. A medical examination is necessary.

Burial-vault. It is a good dream, meaning that everything works to aid you. When it is destroyed or is poorly maintained, as well as when you are closed in a burial-vault in a dream, it is advisable to visit a doctor and take measure to guard the family from problems.

Bushes. Bushes of any kind forecast obstacles in business. To hide in the bushes means inevitable death.

Butcher. A dream with a presence of a butcher is unfavorable. If the butcher is working with meat, it means the need for a medical exam.

Candle. A clear, well-lighted candle on the table forecasts recovery and health for the sick. And for the single – a marriage coming soon. To see an extinguished candle indicates illness; a smoking flame of a candle points to sadness and sickness. To light the candle oneself means the birth of children; while to blow it out means the death of children.

Cannon. To hear or to see a cannon shot forecasts lasting, but not a fatal illness.

Caress. A mother, caressing her child in a dream means that the baby will soon become sick with one of the generally known serious child illnesses. Days and nights of care will bring recovery.

Carrots. Carrots in a dream signal disease.

Castanets. The sound of these instruments presupposes physical disruption in the body. A doctor's consultation is necessary.

Celery. To eat celery in a dream is the symbol of your health and energy up to old age.

Cheeks. To see cheeks that are full and crimson signals success and well-being, while pale and waning cheeks forecast troubles, illnesses, or complications in business.

Cherries. A cherry-tree without cherries is an excellent sign for happiness and good health. Cherries on the tree foretell problems in business. Ripe cherries in a vase mean success in love. To eat sour cherries means tears.

Choking. The effort of swallowing a stuck object or choking in a dream signifies an upset stomach from time to time. Attention to one's diet will help during middle age.

Clothes. To see oneself dressed in red clothes points to blood or blood discharge.

Consternation. To feel consternation in a dream, generally pinpoints the onset of internal problems. A visit to the doctor is recommended.

Cough. To see oneself with a spasmodic cough in the dream indicates good lungs; however, there is a probability of a fit of gout or rheumatism.

Cradle. An empty cradle means arising complications due to poor health. A broken crib for a mother means the sickness or possible death of her child, which can be prevented by continuous guidance over the sick.

Cream. To eat sweet cream in a dream means the onset of dental problems during several months or years, requiring the efforts of a qualified dentist.

Cuckoo-bird. To see a Cuckoo-bird in a dream signals health and welfare.

Cucumbers. For a healthy person, to see and eat cucumbers in a dream forecasts sadness and the destruction of his plans. For a sick person means rapid recovery.

Cup. To drink from a clean cup means health and activity. To drink from a dirty one means the opposite.

Daisy. To see daisies signals illness for women, and displeasure for men.

Dawn. To see a sunset in a dream presages illness; while to see the morning dawn signifies health and welfare.

Death. To see a spirit of a dead relative or friend in a dream means long life with good health and easy circumstances. To see oneself dead is to work for someone with power, to be affluent and have a long life. For the married, it is the forecast of children who will perform all of their responsibilities and you will be comfortable with them. To see a person dead in a dream who is still alive according to your knowledge means that he has carried a message from God to you, which must be heard. To dream that a dead person takes with him something pertaining to you is the symbol of your own death or the death of your friend or relative.

Decanter. To see oneself drinking wine or beer from a decanter signifies approaching indifference to habits and to taste. Problems associated with the liver or stomach will from time to time remind of themselves.

Diarrhea. A premonition of illness, grief and loss.

Dirt. To walk on dirt in a dream is the symbol of sickness. To see oneself or your clothes in dirt, i.e. being untidy, means sickness, hassle, and recommendation to have a medical exam.

Dizziness. To observe growing dizziness during dancing is the forerunner of your health growing worse. You will catch a cold or flu.

Donkey. A donkey kicking you in a dream is the forerunner of a serious or even fatal illness.

Dough. To mix dough signifies good health and nutrition.

Drinking. Drinking oil in a dream means illness dealing with poisoning. To drink hot water, illness and problems. To drink water with unpleasant odor, a sign of rage. A drink in unlimited quantity means that you will recover from one of the forms of anger. To drink water from a fountain or a spring is another sign of illness.

Dropsy. To have dropsy in a dream means the aggravation of one's health because of diabetes. First, you will have good health for a long time before diabetes onset.

Eagle-owl. To see this bird in a dream forecasts misfortune.

Eggs. To see eggs in a dream is usually a good sign. To eat eggs in moderation foretells good health or its improvement if you are not well. To eat them without any limit forecasts harm and illness.

Entrails. This is a warning that it is necessary to decrease the load of any kind, to avoid all the situations causing anxiety, and the need for immediate consultation with a physician.

Epidemic. This dream points to a psychological problem, possibly linked with organic transformations. A consultation with a specialist is necessary.

Eyes. To have many eyes or to look quickly with them in a dream means success and welfare. To see the eyes in an improper place signifies blindness to the person who has had this dream. To lose one or both eyes means sickness or the death of children.

Fainting. A dream where you lose your consciousness is very sad. If it happens on a lively street, be alert for infectious disease. If it is in a place of entertainment, try to show maximal care about your partner or loved one.

Festival. Involvement in a dream of some annual celebration means that you will soon have to care for a sick child. You will soon suffer from headaches or the loss of a close friend.

Fire. The people who see fire in a dream are often endowed with a fierce temper. To see a calm fire without smoke in the fireplace or another spot means excellent health. A flame blowing out by itself is the forerunner of sickness and other difficulties. A fire started which is impossible to maintain forecasts death for the sick person. To see oneself in flames foretells illness, often fever; but to see another person in flames, the death of the one in flames. To see one's bed burning with flames indicates damage, illness or death of one's spouse. To see fire sparks falling from the sky is a specially dangerous symbol for the individual – a forerunner of

a fatal accident.

Fish. To see a lot of big fish is the symbol of good health and being. To see fish of different colors and sizes signals complications in illness for the sick. To catch sea fish in a dream is a bad sign.

Fleas. A dream in which one kills several fleas says that there is no need to worry. The presence of a large number of fleas signals lasting illness.

Flour. A purchase of flour means illness or death of a close friend.

Flowers. A dream that you are picking flowers means great happiness. To hold flowers or to smell them in an unusual situation means grief or even death. To gather or smell field flowers means sadness, weakening of body and reason. Red flowers are usually a messenger of illness, or even death.

Fog. To see fog in a dream forecasts sickness which will pass soon.

Fruits. A sick person seeing a collection of various fruits in a dream will soon recover.

Girl. For a man to be a girl in a dream means concealed sexual problems. Visiting a psychotherapist is recommended.

Goose. To see a goose in an aviary is the advice to maintain one's diet. In the case of normal weight, one should check the blood pressure and blood sugar.

Gout. To see gout affecting the hands in a dream means chest pain, fear, and potential trauma for the young. A visit to the physician is recommended. For the aged, it is the lack of energy, insufficiency of material resources, sickness, and sometimes death.

Grapes. To dream about grapes is a factor of sadness. To eat dry grapes or to harvest grapes means sadness, tears, and loss.

Grass. To see green grass in a dream forecasts the fulfilment of all hopes and wishes, and recovery for the sick. Seeing wilted grass presages illness. If a sick person sees cut grass in a dream, it foretells death; and for the healthy person, bad luck. To eat grass or herbs in a dream is to have good health and long life. To smell aromatic herbs means sadness and weakness for everyone, excluding the doctor.

Hair. Well-groomed hair means health. To see a woman without hair is disease; while to see a man without hair means health and welfare. To cut one's own hair in a dream leads to unexpected sadness, misfortune, or even illness. To have fur in the dream instead of hair signals disease.

Handcuffs. To see handcuffs in a dream is the worst sign for those married, as it means illness, termination of business, and jail. For a single person, it means marriage.

Hawk. To see a hawk in a dream foretells a lasting and

dangerous, and often fatal, illness. To shoot a hawk means tranquillity, a favorable incident.

Head. To see a gray head in dream means joy and respect. To cut off a head of a bird in a dream signals recovery for the sick, while for others it means success in their business. To see one's head of diminished proportions, strangely shaped, is the sign of retardation or other problems.

Heart. If, in a dream, someone is having a pain in the heart, it is the symbol of dangerous illness. Not to have or to lose the heart in a dream signifies sudden death. To see an unusually enlarged or palpitating heart forecasts a dangerous illness.

Hiccups. This dream usually has a physical origin and warns about alcohol abuse.

House. Painting one's house in a dream means illness in the family.

Illness. To see oneself sick in a dream means illness for a healthy person, but recovery for the sick one.

Insanity. To be insane in a dream forecasts recovery for a sick person, while to the disconsolate one – consolation from sadness. To see oneself behaving crazily in public places signifies that you will live long, will be a favorite and an influential person.

Insect. To kill insects in a dream indicates illness.

Insurance. To receive a refusal of medical insurance in a dream symbolizes a long and happy life.

Intestines. To see intestine in a dream shows a form of ailment or anxiety. If the dream includes the sensation of pain, it is necessary to see a doctor as soon as possible.

Ivy. This is a very good dream, and one of its meanings is good health and happiness.

Jam. To eat jam in a dream foretells short-term sickness.

Joking. To joke in a dream means to grieve in reality.

Kidneys. To see one's own kidneys presupposes a medical exam.

Kitchen. A dream about a cluttered or dirty kitchen is a signal about a needed medical exam.

Knees. If you see your knees tired or swollen, it signifies sickness or other ripening problems.

Laboratory. To see a laboratory in a dream means danger and illness.

Lake. To be out on the lake during stormy weather is the sign of forthcoming serious illness, which will not constitute a permanent impact on your good destiny.

Leaves. To see falling leaves in a dream forecasts a dangerous illness.

Legs. To have light and agile legs for dancing means health, good disposition and joy. Washing one's legs forecasts trouble or breast disease. To see one's legs swollen is the premonition of illness or death of friends. To see oneself having three or four legs pinpoints a problem in the legs. To see the calves of the leg big and soft means illness or an obstacle. To see legs full of blood signals a healthy and fortunate life, not only for the dreamer, but also for his whole family.

Lips. To have beautiful lips in a dream is the sign that your friends are healthy, but if the lips are dry, then it is the opposite. To have fine, big lips in a dream indicates that you will have outstanding children. Sick lips presage illness in kids or relatives.

Liver. If someone is complaining about his or her liver in a dream, then his or her money will vanish and he or she will suddenly die.

Marriage. To see oneself married in a dream means illness, melancholy, insecure future, or even death.

Meeting. To meet a man in a dream means success in endeavors, while to meet a woman means obstacles. To meet a person who has died in a dream is the sign of disease, or even death.

Melon. For a sick person to see a melon in a dream is considered to recover soon.

Mint. For sick persons, this herb signifies recovery; and for the healthy ones, happiness.

Mirror. For the healthy person to look in the mirror, forecasts disease, while for the sick one, death. A broken mirror in a dream means sad news and a difficult period of life in the future.

Moon. To see a moon in a dream means to possess health, love and well-being. To see a shaded moon in a dream indicates illness or death for the woman in your family.

Motor. To stand next to a working motor means the loss of physical strength through illness.

Mushrooms. To see growing mushrooms means health and long life. To gather mushrooms in a dream presages well-being and a high place in society.

Nakedness. To see oneself naked in a dream means illness and troubles. To be naked in a bath signals joy and pleasure. To see an unfamiliar person naked in a dream is the sign of being suddenly scared.

Name. To hear your name pronounced in a dream foretells troubles or death.

Neck. To see one's own neck swollen is a sign of illness.

Ointment. To prepare ointment in a dream means anxiety and difficulties – an approach of insignificant sickness; nothing serious.

Olives. To see olives on a tree signals recovery for the sick and love with friendship for the rest. The olive tree in some cases signifies death, but mainly, just as the laurel tree, it is the symbol of success.

Organ. To hear the music of an organ in a church indicates that you will be seriously sick and this will undoubtedly touch upon your way of life.

Oysters. To eat oysters in a dream serves as a good sign in all areas. It is a symbol of good health.

Pain. A regular pain sensation is either a physical pain or the need to visit a doctor.

Palace. To be inside a palace or to see it from the outside indicates a discomfiture or shock which your health will experience for a short period.

Pantyhose. To put on woolen stockings means joy and abundance; silk stockings, poverty; cotton, mediocre state. To take them off signifies sadness. To be in torn pantyhose means sadness, misfortune, or even death.

Paralysis. To be seized by paralysis in a dream shows that the cardiovascular system is not properly functioning. A waning of spiritual disposition and of general physical state will pursue you until you ingest iron and other necessary ingredients in food. Generally, this disorder occurring in a dream, no matter who the person is, presupposes emotional conflict or sexual obstacles. Partial paralysis reveals fear of frigidity, impotence, or concealed homosexuality. It can also mean a suppressed desire for liberation from a physical ailment. Advice from a doctor or a psychotherapist would be useful.

Path. To see oneself strolling along a nice path means health.

Pencil. Good health, good luck, even if they are sold in a dream.

Peonies. To see this flower in a dream signifies anxiety and irritation. A visit to the doctor will be useful.

Pepper. To grind pepper in a dream points to melancholy.

Pig. To see a live or dead pig is not good. To sell or buy pigs means sickness.

Pike. To see a pike in a dream signifies illness.

Pillow. To see the pillow of your armchair torn is the sign that you might have strong pain in your waist area. A consultation from a good doctor is necessary.

Plums. To eat plums in a dream signals illness.

Pneumonia. A warning about the need for medical exam.

Pond. For a married woman, to see a pond in a dream points to pregnancy in the near future. If there is a lot of fish in the pond, she will have twins. If the fish are small, the next child will be a boy. For a widow, it means a happy marriage.

Quarantine. A misfortune is waiting for you in the future if you do not take care of your health.

Rabbit. To see a rabbit in a dream is the weakening of health, while to eat a rabbit is good health.

Rash. To see a rash in a dream in one of the body parts means sickness from overcooling, bronchitis, or inflammation of the lungs. The period of sickness will not be prolonged.

Reading. Reading fiction in a dream means joy and consolation. Reading spiritual literature forecasts happiness, both physically and spiritually.

Rope. To see oneself in a dream tied with a rope or a string means that one will suffer from a serious ailment.

Roses. To see in a dream roses blooming in one's house means welfare and joy for the healthy, and death for the sick. To see roses in an unusual time has an opposite meaning. Red roses means joy and pleasant news.

Salt. To see salt in a dream is the sign of wisdom, but to eat it indicates illness.

Seaweed. To see seaweed in a dream bends towards displeasure. To get tangled in seaweed means a dangerous illness and troubles.

Sexual Organs. A dream in which the sexual organs are bared means that you are on the verge of dangerous sexual problems. One should ask for professional advice. A dream about pain in this area means a need to visit a doctor.

Shark. This dream signifies the end to a serious problem or illness.

Shoes. To see nice-looking shoes in a dream means well-being and recognition. Untidy or poor quality shoes mean illness and shame.

Silence. Absolute quietude or unusual silence pre-supposes a hidden nervous shock. It is necessary to visit a doctor.

Silver. If a pregnant woman sees silver in a dream, it means that she will give birth to a girl and the procedure will go smoothly, but the child will not be rich. To look on silver means danger from sickness if measures for cleanliness are not taken.

Singing. A person singing in a dream will have a reason to cry. For a sick person, hearing the singing or music indicates recovery.

Sky. To see a clear and light sky signals recovery for the sick and, for the rest, a fulfilment of their wishes. An overcast sky means sickness and bad luck in any endeavor.

Snake. To see a snake in a dream denotes imminent danger, sickness, betrayal or hatred. To kill the snake in a dream is to overcome all obstacles and gain victory over enemies.

Sneezing. To see oneself sneezing in a dream means health.

Spring. To see in a dream a spring of pure water forecasts health for the sick person and abundance for the healthy one. If the water is turbid and impure, the dream has the opposite meaning.

Spitting. To see oneself spat at in a dream forecasts recovery for the sick, but illness and abuse for the healthy.

Staircase. To descend down the stairs means sickness or poor health.

Stallion. You might hear the news about the birth of a child.

Star. To see a star falling onto the roof of your house means illness; the house will be empty or destroyed by the flames. The star glowing inside the house is the warning about a fatal danger to the owner of the household.

Stick. To walk with a stick in a dream means illness.

Strawberries. For a pregnant woman, the dream containing strawberries presages a birth of a boy. For a girl, it means marriage to a man who will be affluent and will

make her happy. For a man, it means a pleasant wife with whom he will have many children.

Stroke. To see oneself having a stroke points to possible functional problems in the body. A visit to the doctor is recommended. To see someone else affected with a stroke means news about illness.

Stomach. A feeling of pain in the area of the stomach in a dream points to future success with the aid of good health and energetic activity.

Suffocation. A dream about a real physical transformation in the body. Asthma is a possibility. Doctor's advice is recommended.

Swan. To see a swan in a dream means a happy family life and many children who will be successful and will live long and happily.

Swimming. Swimming in a dream indicates heavy toil, sadness and sickness, especially if the head is placed below the water level.

Sword. To see a clear and clean sword in a dream presages health and body strength.

Table. It means joy if you see a table in a dream, but if you lay it with dishes, a sign of abundance. To see a broken table in a dream means sickness for your wife, and sometimes, her death.

Teeth. A new, growing tooth is an addition to the family. The presence of rotten or decaying tooth, the death of a relative or friend. A tooth falling out with blood means the loss of a close relative. Shaking teeth, a sign of sickness.

Temperature. A dream in which you have a higher than normal temperature means that, for some time, you will not suffer from serious illness.

Thirst. The feeling of unquenchable thirst is the sign of great sadness. To quench the feeling of thirst with clear, fresh water is to have health and well-being. To quench the thirst with turbid or unfresh water leads towards disappointment and possibly towards light illness.

Throat. To see in a dream one's inflamed throat indicates disease. To see one's throat cut with a knife means that you will be wounded by someone. To cut the throat of your friend means that you will hurt him or her somehow.

Tongue. To have a wounded tongue in a dream foretells sickness for a wife or a close relative.

Towel. A short sickness with rapid recovery.

Tree. To see green, blooming or ripe trees in a dream is a good sign. To plant trees in a dream is the birth of a child or marriage. To see oneself transformed into a tree forecasts disease.

Turkey. This bird brings a warning about illness. Take care of your health, otherwise you'll have serious problems.

Ugliness. To be ugly in a dream is the sign of an illness or sadness. It is very good sign for the dreamer to see an ugly person in his dream.

Venom. To see venom in a dream signifies dangerous illness, death or epidemic.

Watch. A watch that has stopped means that you will be involved in sickness or business losses. To see a broken watch is specially dangerous for the sick. The watch running ahead of time presages death, while one running behind, a sign of long life.

Water. To see clear water means welfare, while seeing turbid water, sadness. Cold water is toward health; warm water toward illness. Boiling water suggests death after a long illness.

Watermelon. For a sick person, eating a watermelon in a dream signals recovery, while for the healthy person, sadness.

Wax. To see wax in a dream signals illness for a healthy person, while it means death for a sick one.

Window. To see closed windows in a dream is favorable to family affairs. To see a house without windows is death to one of the family members.

Wine. To see wine in a dream is a bad sign. To drink clear wine forecasts health and success. To drink wine mixed with water means an inevitable sickness. To see yourself drinking wine means that your health will soon suffer from neglecting one's responsibilities.

Wings. To have wings in a dream or to fly is the sign of recovery for the sick, while for the healthy person, it is the acquisition of all favors.

Woman. To see in a dream a woman or wife indicates disease. To see a dark-haired woman presages dangerous illness, while for a sick person to see a blond woman may lead to death. To see a woman with a light-colored face means recovery for the sick person.

Chapter XII

HEALING

ETHICS

The man must pass through a wide field of trials and experience, stand up to face the unexpected dangers and unknown forces, which he must overcome, as in this battle you neither ask for mercy nor you are given one.

— The Culture of Concentration

The Law of Time and Space

The life is short and time is long,
Do what you can to live in the world,
You must survive to be the best,
This is the law of time and space.

To be born is step number one,
To live and be in this old cruel world,
You are not alone but you think to yourself,
This is the law of time and space.

To go to school is step number two,
To learn new things and to meet new friends,
You go with people you love and you hate,
This is the law of time and space.

To go and do what you can is step number three,
To make and break some lives and hopes,
You see and hear the lies and the truth,
This is the law of time and space.

To live life to the fullest is step number four,
The future is near and your time is at hand,
The time has come to go you know not where,
This is the law of time and space.

N. Madorsky

From the moment my healing practice expanded beyond the boundaries of my family and friends, the problem of ethics became a stumbling block for me. How can one act and behave in such delicate situations when, after getting a glimpse of the person you are talking to, you discover through your nature-granted gift that this person is seriously ill? Should you tell the person about it? Such a dilemma was posed more than once for me. More than once I have regretted that I have neither warned someone about a problem, nor tried to attract attention to the fact. It is especially painful and remorseful to realize that time cannot be turned backwards.

I will never forget my father's return from the doctor with the news that his blood pressure was normal and that there were no problems with his health. While we were talking about the results of his visit to the doctor, I noticed clear blood-filled dots in the corner of his right eye and instantly felt that a stroke was imminent. I couldn't understand why the doctor didn't notice it during his examination. I couldn't give warning to my father because he was so full of hope at that moment.

After a couple of weeks, he suffered a stroke. Later, I shared with him what I had spotted earlier. His reaction was that he wouldn't have taken it seriously anyway after the assurance from the doctor. If this was the reaction of a person close to me, then what could be expected from those who I happened to meet or who came to see me for the first time?

In due time, I started to regard and guard carefully any messages with unfavorable content. Still, I consider it my duty to hint about being on the alert, which allows him or her, upon evaluation, to alleviate the critical situation or to postpone indefinitely the inevitable outcome. The opportunity to receive an early warning gives one a chance and a choice to gain victory over the disease or to retreat from the struggle, choosing an easier way – to leave life as it is. To decide what to do with the obtained information is the task of the patient.

In one way or another, from this time on, the clock is actually starting to tick backwards. Life is an endless chain of continuous fighting for one's health. To be healthy constitutes an enormous effort, the goal of one's whole life. No one else but you can take the responsibility for your health. Why people themselves are sometimes reluctant to be responsible for their own fate, a reason that would be easy to confide to the physician or to family and friends, is difficult for me to understand.

Let me give you an example from a recent experience. I met Charles at a seminar on nutrition. At the end of the seminar one of my patients, who was present at this event decided to demonstrate the capabilities of and differences between various methods of diagnosis. Asking me to describe briefly the essence of my method, he then invited Charles to be tested by me, for no particular reason. Demonstrating no-contact diagnosis, I mentioned some of the problems in his body, but I didn't reveal other problems due to ethical considerations. Then, for the first time in my healing practice, I asked Charles to lie down in front of the whole group and showed that he was in actuality experiencing a strong imbalance of his energy centers.

Then another healer was called on who employed a somewhat different method of discovering deviations from the norm. All of the disorders named by me were confirmed, but with one difference. He could not give – or maybe he is not endowed with it – one of the unpleasant diagnoses. Possibly he didn't wish to pursue it.

Before leaving, I asked Charles whether someone in his family was affected with cancer. It happened that his mother died from cancer of the ovaries. Then I gave him my business card and recommended that he pray and drink green tea.

Charles called the next day and asked for an emergency visit. Our conversation, to my surprise, lasted more than three hours. With apparent interest, he asked what terrible thing I had found in him, to make me tell him that it is time to ask the Lord for assistance. So I diagnosed him with cancer of the rectum.

Charles was quite surprised that I didn't say anything about the kidneys because he had felt pain there for some time. But the kidneys were only undergoing some inflammatory process. Actually, Charles sensed something wrong with his rectum two years ago when he had noticed a drop of blood in his excrement. At this time, he had rushed to see the doctor, but a complete medical exam did not confirm his fears.

Two years later somebody who has seen him for the first time gives a diagnosis of the condition which he already subconsciously knew was present in his body. What can one do in such situation? Trust one's intuition, the healer, or the doctor?

I repeated the diagnostic procedure with the same result – no changes for the better. I showed him and explained the difference between a healthy and sick organism from the perspective of bioenergetics. It is very difficult to accept the signal of warning about the danger, especially in cases connected with cancer.

Only in rare cases are people not overtaken by a great feeling of fear when the word "cancer" is pronounced aloud. Moreover, upon hearing such news, people are not usually very willing to take responsibility for themselves in fighting cancer. I was told that he had to consult with his wife about his future actions because she does not believe in "such tales," and without her, Charles could not decide. In any case, he has to take responsibility for himself now. I gave him a deadline before which I could help him. After it expires, he must rely only on himself and on the best doctor in the world – God.

Here's another example: Lora began to attend my healing sessions, soon felt better and discontinued them, and took advice from the doctor about taking a medicine which is known to disable the regenerative activity of the immune system. She made a choice.

We still do not realize that nothing accidental happens in nature. Everything has its ruling principle at a given period of time. If you have received a painful signal – attend to it. Pause for a while. Think. Maybe it's not a haphazard sharp pinching, but a deeply hidden chronic or oncological disease. Respect your health and cherish your body.

Is it ethical not to care for your personal health? We are only given one life at a time and must learn to value this priceless gift. It is highly immoral to treat oneself as an unnecessary object.

Why are students in medical schools not taught how to protect themselves from psychological or emotional stress? Physicians must know how to use their mind to build an imaginary shield like a glass wall around their bodies or other techniques as well.

Ethics! What can you do when a former patient, Keith, whom you saved from death at a time when all his relatives and doctors dismissed his chances of survival, is informed a couple years later about the presence of a problem other than cancer? You can caution him about the danger, but you know for sure that, in this situation, you cannot help him as the window has closed. On the one hand, he has completed his mission with his family, but on the other hand, he has not learned from the previous experience to change his attitude toward the people around him and to reconsider his spiritual values.

I am not sure how you, the reader, would have acted in my place, but I used my courage to inform him of my suspicions. Checking his energy field, I discovered I was right: functional disorders of the heart. I tried to focus Keith's attention to the seriousness of his situation, advising him to decrease his physical load and enjoy all the pleasures of life for his remaining segment of time. I acted the same way as my parents did when the final days of their loved ones were approaching, and the way I will want others to act toward me. We must not pass on our unfinished business to those remaining after us in this intriguing, and mystery-filled world. Each following generation fulfils its own unique mission.

A few hours after my meeting with Keith, he called. On the phone, I heard something that is not easily retold – it was a scream, the scream of a desperate individual, not believing, that having been liberated once from the claws of death, he again found himself in its embrace. This was an individual unwilling to transform spiritually, accusing me and everyone else of his blunders. Months later, he sent me a letter with good advice, a sign of hidden apology.

While investigating the interconnection of generations in families of patients from the perspective of genetic links, you come, against your will, to a paradoxical conclusion. Nothing goes unchecked; everything is registered by certain sensors, applied to personal affairs, and analyzed by invisible scientists, and then some superpowerful processor spits out the consequences of life's actions.

I will try to narrate a classic situation of a triangle. Geraldine came to me because of depression connected with her husband. She could not tolerate his attempts at self-discovery, beginning with the study of philosophy and ending with a visit to a healer. Geraldine was considering the last remedy, divorce. She struggled with what she saw as his breach with reality and decided she could not cope with her problem alone. The first visit she made, on her husband's advice, was to his healer, after which she came to see me.

Soon their situation became clear. Her husband, in the initial stages of cancer, was under the influence of his subconscious. He was blindly searching for ways of deliverance from his disease, the existence of which he did not yet suspect. He loved his wife in the depth of his soul but he became immersed in the karmic cycle of his healer. The tragedy had unfolded according to all guidelines of theater, but it was not to be played out to the end!

The restored energy fields in Geraldine influenced the energy shells of her husband, which forced him to search further for the truth. However, Geraldine's actions were almost neutralized by the combined efforts of her spouse and his instructing healer. In this situation, I saw the impact of karmic forces, proceeding from one of his previous lives into the present reincarnation in order to give Geraldine a lesson. The main idea for her is that in the struggle of two vital forces, there are always the victors and the vanquished. It is her decision. The answer to questions about the cause of the relationship change in her family and relatives has almost been found. Now she needs to spend some time analyzing the complexity of the situation.

The above-mentioned healer had broken the laws of ethics while trying to achieve her goals in healing. She allowed her own individual motives to enter into the constructive work of the higher forces. Thus, she became a victim of karma's law herself. While she was endowed with healing gifts, she started to practice prior to her time of spiritual maturity. She had affairs with her clients. Karmic links between spouses are formed before birth, and no one – including healers and spiritual leaders – is ordained to change them. All are forbidden to interfere with the higher aims of creation.

Many healers find their way to me by one way or another. They always pose the same question: "Why, if I can help others, am I not able to help myself?" They frequently visit me when traditional medicine is not able to help. But it is never too late. It is difficult to perceive with one's soul that not everyone is granted the right to cure and not everyone has natural defenses. While everything has its meaning, not everyone can grasp it. When using their natural abilities, healers are often bewildered by the astounding results, which they didn't even dream about. Seeing the products of their actions, they forget that they are mortals. Any diseases – both acquired or inherited, as well as the karmic – can overtake us which no one can really evade. We cannot ensure ourselves against punishment while transgressing against the Ten Commandments. We, healers, must remember that our unique gift is the same as that of an artist or composer and no one has the right to elevate oneself above God.

From my personal observations, I see that only people with a kind soul and pure, loving heart, those openly willing to help the afflicted, can have access to healing. In some cases, a conversation with the sufferer is sufficient to make him feel better. At such moments, the healing energy is emitted from the healer towards the one in need and there is no need for special tactics. The sick are transformed in front of one's eyes: they grow younger; their eyes light up and emit a special light of life; beautiful smiles appear on their faces. Each time I see this released divine light, my heart is filled with an unusual feeling of delight for what has been accomplished. If he/she is not born with the healing art and not spiritually mature, the practitioner is taking a risk by invading the sphere of the unknown which is locked to most people.

I consider an invasion of the subconscious to be the greatest sin, as the subconscious is in charge of not only the present, but also carries responsibility for the future. One of these effects on the thinking activity of a human being is the use of the power of hypnosis. Although treatment by hypnosis is quite widespread, it is a violation of the privacy of our subconscious. A purposeful destruction of individuality can occur at the level of the subconscious. No one has the right to tamper with our subconscious because it is where the will of God resides. Initially, we may believe that hypnosis has helped us for some period of time. Later, our subconscious will wrestle for control over of the situation. Before regaining control, we remain divided on the subconscious level.

After exiting the state of hypnosis, the subconscious begins the internal invisible struggle with the externally implanted forces, trying to control its field of activity and its allotted mission. An identity split unnoticeable to us occurs. There is a face which we observe every minute, but there is also one hidden from our eyes as well as from the patient under hypnosis.

The destruction of personality happens indiscernibly, becoming dependent on the commands given by the controlling person. Such hypnotists mask their abilities under the facade of a kind and sensitive nature. Unfortunately, it is only a facade. They often resemble a smooth-tongued, fondling pussy-cat, purring, while people imperceptibly become subservient to them. Great efforts for the individual are required for liberation. Nothing is given out freely – you have to pay for everything sooner or later. The price for using hypnotism could be the loss of one's identity.

My experience shows that patients who earlier have tried the curative power of hypnosis cannot extract themselves from its fetters, even after they don't need it. The ongoing effect of hypnosis does not give you a chance to make an individual decision when you are alone with your problem and there is nobody else to solve it. This refers especially to the patients who have very serious diseases, who are dependent on medications, drinking, drugs, or nervous complications – and are unable to assert themselves.

Hypnosis and healing trances are two different states. In my practice, I never use hypnosis to manipulate the consciousness and subconsciousness of my patient's mind. A healing trance appears when a person feels my energy around his body or when I hold my palms over specific areas of their body. The trance can be light, where he feels and remembers everything around him or his psychic vision. The trance may be very deep where he will remember only his psychic vision or nothing. His experience depends on the condition of his health and how he is connected to the Quasiworld or what kind of healing is going on in his body.

A healing trance never leaves patients depending on the will of the healer. If a person had been hypnotized at some time before, I will feel it, whether or not I touch his head. This type of person is very interesting to treat because I never know what will happen with his mind. Today he might want to be treated and tomorrow nobody knows. I prefer to treat people whose mind works clearly and who know what they want in life without outside pressure.

One story after another, each unique, all have something in common – their karmic consequences. Most of these stories touch upon families experiencing manifestations of cancer. Using modern technology and longer life expectancy, these cases can be registered and analyzed. It makes one shiver to think how all of us are interconnected and interlaced with energy fields and affected by the exchange of information; not just on the visible level, but also on the atomic and metaphysical levels.

We cannot change the laws of nature but we are capable of absorbing them and successfully adapting to them. The main idea to grasp and accept with one's soul is that: the laws are eternal and immobile and that the smallest transgression is returned according to rules of the universe. They are as old as mankind itself and have served as the primary fuel of our existence on the earth.

Opening the Bible, people learn that they don't have to look for anything new; everything has been known since the ancient times, and we are simply repeating another coil of the spiral in assimilating what had been assimilated by the previous generations of sages.

"I the Lord am your God.

You shall have no other gods besides Me.

For I the Lord your God, visiting the

guilt of the parents upon the children

upon the third and upon the fourth

generations of those who reject Me.

You shall not 'swear falsely

by' the name of the Lord your God."

"Honor your parents and respect your neighbors."

"You shall not murder or commit suicide."

"Do unto others as you would have them do unto you."

I would love to stress that for a modern man the necessity of living in harmony with Nature is also very urgent

So, what can be done from the ethical point of view? Tell the truth or conceal it? Consider it moral to inform one of the inevitable end, even if there is a solution to prolong life in this situation? Does the doctor who insinuates to the patient the information about terminal illness behave morally from the ethical point of view, or does he transgress the laws of humanity? Is it ethical to tell the true diagnosis or to hide it, as some doctors do nowadays, fearing reaction from insurance companies or the rage of the patient? How can you call it ethics? What can you do about ethics, when already knowing the influence of one or another medication, you still prescribe it and thus destroy the immune system completely? Whether it will help or not, whether or not improvement will occur, whether the patient will live or not, you must treat the questions of health scrupulously and with care.

I remember reading some good advice from Leo Tolstoy: "A human being is always making plans, deceiving himself. But one must also bravely confront the destruction of one's plans."

Chapter XIII

SEARCH FOR THE TRUTH

Life is not a static thing. The only people who do not change their minds are incompetents in asylums, who can't, and those in cemeteries.

—Everett Dirksen

Upon finishing this book, I realize a lot of my experiences will not be illustrated here, for to encompass everything is not possible. Each day and each new patient bring something previously unknown or long-forgotten. I am not aware of all of the intricacies of healing, but I have realized that the abilities given from birth require to be used and constantly perfected. Not using talents leads to undesirable consequences for those who have them.

I confronted many similar situations because there is nothing unique and unparalleled in the sphere of human relationships in the world. But every one of us is an unparalleled pearl of Nature – with a coating made unique by the Creator.

The real stories I told in this book hopefully will help to determine your attitude toward disease and to find the meaning in your life, and to help you make the right choices to live life to its fullest. It is necessary to view each disease as a lesson from which we can learn.

Acquiring the ability to recover is similar to developing the will to pursue self-education. To force oneself to change a habitual way of life, which demands perpetual exertion and daily struggles with one's disease and the spiritual enemy – an inert struggles with one's disease and the spiritual enemy – an inert subconscious, which was adapted over the years according to one's needs – is not an easy task.

The first step on the road of resistance against disease is the beginning of your self-education. Each painful sensation is the impetus towards the knowledge of the new, which asks for some strength in the search for the truth. Each time you ask yourself a question: "Why is it me and why does some terrible fate force me to seek ways of deliverance?" Each new step in the search for the answer to the questions means another step toward healing.

Knowledge of the anatomical and physiological structure of one's own body leads to the discovery of ways to deliverance through nontraditional healing. Who, besides you, must love yourself and your own body most of all? Your body demands knowledge which will help it to cope with disaster, and you are its only assistant. Knowledge, accumulated through millennia, is in your hands once you manifest curiosity. From where it comes doesn't matter; it is the result that is most important. Your recovery or prevention of disease depends only on you. The unwillingness to preserve oneself and desire to be surrounded by the approval of loved ones are premises towards being defeated in the yet unstarted battle.

Often we do not have the strength alone to deal with the overwhelming disaster, but we must not lose courage. A little more effort and you will be rewarded. Your attending physician or the recommended healer will become your conductor in the search for paths to healing. However, no one can confront it better than you can!

Our diseases often begin before our birth or pursue us from our previous lives. Some methods of establishing the marked disorders of fate, which our grandfathers and great-grandfathers have used, are listed in this book. The dreams and the palm lines of the hand are material which everyone can use alone. Such inquiry does not require any contrivances or disguises. The book provides you with primary knowledge, but the rest depends on you.

However, if we still continue to doubt in our soul – then, there comes a time of contact between our conscious and subconscious minds. We have some information about one of the oldest devices employed by the ancient oracles. It is a common pendulum, an indicator of our omniscient subconscious, for which there exists nothing that is unknown.

Conversing with our subconscious, we find out the reason for our physical state, and then, we continue the search for elimination of illness. If necessary, the traditional methods using medicine and surgery can be of service. However, at the same time, one can also employ the old ways of healing, such as herbs, charms, breathing exercises, acupuncture, or the use of special invisible forces through those unique individuals, the healers.

Various temptations are awaiting you here. To get onto this secure path, you can receive a hint from your own body, which subconsciously knows the only unmistakable ways toward recovery that are going to be successful, despite the various opinions of your relatives.

Trust your subconscious. It will prompt you to make the right choice, and your chosen healer-guide, who, for a time will become an intermediary between you and the Higher Forces of nature, and will be your teacher. Each representative of the science of healing has extraordinary abilities which were developed as a result of practice. Not every healer has the right from above to cure cancer or other serious illnesses and, thus, to correct karma.

In such cases, it is advisable to consult the psychic visionaries to confirm the accuracy of your choice. Although you may think yourself fortunate that you found the right healer, don't rush to rejoice. Finding a healer doesn't mean that you are ready to endure the struggle with yourself. The initiated course of treatment needs to be completed. You cannot stop halfway. If you interrupt the course of treatment, the positive microcellular transformations, cut off from their source of support, will return to their old configurations, to the beginning of disease.

During healing, numerous contacts with the Higher Forces occur, with whom you'll have to maintain good relationships. They lead to a change in your way of thinking and your behavior in regard to relatives and colleagues, as well as the spiritual condition and your attitude toward the higher forces of the universe and your quasi-friends.

The spiritual growth of a human being is the biggest victory over the dark forces of nature. Internal spiritual purification is necessary not only for those in search of the righteous path, but also for those who have grasped the meaning of life at the moment of confession and fusion with this mystical Quasiworld which has attracted people throughout millennia.

The road to the Truth is captivating because it passes through self-knowledge, which amounts to the highest rapture – to the self-healing of the spirit, and then the body, as its physical attribute. Those who find themselves in the service of mankind carry a heavy burden in both moral and material dimensions. The spiritual development and self-perfection doesn't stop for a second. It draws you into a cesspool, from which there is no exit.

Having read this book, people will be tempted to emerge with the announcement about the discovery of their own super-talents and will strive to embellish them to perfection. Perfection does not exist! The eternal search for truth leads to infinity. We are not granted the chance to know everything because we are not ready to receive the information, higher knowledge designated only for the mature community in the highest level of human development. Humanity is at the stage of infancy, so to speak, in which the accumulation of outside information with the acquisition of experience takes place over time and space. So, what is behind the wall? Each revelation in its own time!

My patients and participants in my seminars encouraged me to write this book. I finally realized with all the fibers of my soul, that much is not in our power and does not depend upon us. Life is given to us in its multifaceted dimensions for the purpose of accomplishing some goals. What would happen to us if we were to discover the essence of living in another time and space continuum? Think of the tumult news article creates about something supernatural, which gives us anxiety. Motivation toward understanding the beckoning quasiworld will never stop. Then, the question comes: "Do we need this?"

I would have liked to share much more with you, but I prefer self-education to any other method of learning. I wish you success in your search for knowledge in the boundless world of information. The best way is to practice under the guidance of an expert and a benevolent teacher. Due to my mission and character, I never had the chance to meet someone who might have changed my way of life in my earlier years. I am grateful for my fate.

Faith in yourself is your weapon at all your beginnings – whether it's facing a disease or embracing the appearance of your talents! I have brought you to the edge of consciousness. Now go on with confidence. Best of luck in your search for the truth!

My Words

The tables are standing and the people are sitting.

Nobody is listening to what I have to say.

The floor is made of wood, what kind of wood is the
question I am asking.

No one cares what kind wood the floor is made of.

That's right. Who cares? It is just a floor.

People are talking between themselves about their
lives and how they are.

I don't care as long as I can say what I want to say.

My words will be heard in the air as a sound.

The vibration of my words, the words that I say.

Not everyone listens, many think of something else.

I said what I wanted, inspiring, now time to go.

Nathaniel Madorsky

GLOSSARY

Acupuncture – to influence the body to heal itself by inserting tiny needles into the body in specific invisible points.

Acupuncture points – tiny, invisible, concentrated centers of energy and intellect, located in the nervous system (electrical system or energy system) of the body which distribute its emotional load; treatment on the points to repair the energy system frees the flow, cells normalize, and heal themselves.

Akashic records – (Sanskrit *akasha*, "primary substance", India) that out of which all things are formed; files which holds the picture images of all events, occurrences, and knowledge one has accepted throughout all lives;

Angel – (Greek *angelos*, "*supernatural being*"); (Hebrew *malak*, literally signifies "a person sent, a messenger") an instrument of divine justice, a guide for men of goodwill

Astral body – while a human is alive: the astral body is an invisible, ethereal substance interpenetrating the physical body and extending outward about five to eight inches.

Aura – an invisible, electromagnetic, intelligent energy field completely surrounding an entity, living and nonliving, functioning as a blueprint and battery for that entity

267

Chakra – (Sanskrit) a whirling vortex of concentrated etheric energy; perceived clairvoyanty as a colorful wheel or flower, with hub in the center; invisible attached along the spine, from base to the top of the head.

Channeling – to allow an etheric world intelligence to enter one's mind and impress thoughts upon the consciousness to be spoken aloud, using one's own voice.

Charms – a song, a chant, a verse; used to psychically act upon a living entity, human, animal, or plant, using a compelling magical force with an intent to change its course of action; to use a charm because of its ethereal qualities to raise the vibrations in order to contact etheric world intelligences for psychic information or physical phenomena.

Color visualization – to use the proper color as a point of focus in a visualization exercise; to sent color to the afflicted part of the body for a healing.

Dead Sea Scrolls – a number of leather scrolls, collaborating on the books in the Old Testament of the Bible; found in 1948 in caves on the northwest of Dead Sea.

DeJa Vu – (French, "already seen"); to sense an innate feeling that where one is for the first, one has been before, or meet an individual for the first time and sense that one knows that individual already.

Dowsing rod – an implement designed to use in hands to detect minerals underground, find lost objects, and to answer questions which require a *yes* or *no* reply; instrument can be made from natural wood in a stick or forked branch shape, copper wire.

Ego – (esoteric) representative of the combination of the conscious and subconscious mind; established from all one's past incarnation experiences, this incarnation's past experiences, and one's attitude toward these experiences; *I am I.*

Entity (human entity) – the sum total that a soul-mind has acquired in individuality, making its own rules and its own rate of vibrations; correctly used to mean a deceased person or a live person.

Erysipelas – is contagious disease of the skin. It is sometimes called St. Anthony's fire. Erysipelas usually appears on the face or scalp, but may affect other parts.

Esoteric – pertains no information and knowledge that is better understood by the feeling nature rather than intellect; cannot necessarily be proven by present scientific means, but its value is not discredited for this reason.

Essenian sect – a Jewish sect capable of communicating with etheric world; appeared first in 150 B.C.; knowledge recorded in the Dead Sea Scrolls; a discipline, that Jesus studied.

Faith healing – this confidence that one will be cured comes from a "desire to live"; this desire of the patient allows the treatment she or he chooses to change their body chemistry so the body can heal itself, at the time one is seeking healing; this desire is "faith" or automatic knowing that one will get better.

Hent – a term for the indivisible and unchanging particle, equivalent to the neutrino, carrying an intellectual message between ordinary reality and the Quasiworld.

Incantations – to sing and chant formulaic words, phrases or sounds to special rhythm, which are composed to stir and build psychic energy for manipulation; used for healing another person, distance no barrier; to chant or sing certain secret sacred words and tones that were composed to joint the two brain hemispheres; helps psychic information to flow more easily, and helps send healing energies to others.

Incarnation – pertains to a life spent in physical flesh living on the earth; theory: humans go through a repetitious pattern of living in the etheric world and living on the earth many times.

Intuition – information that one did not know before through education or past experiences, did not logically think out or reason with; comes with or without the help of the etheric world intelligences.

Kabbala – (Hebrew, "doctrines received from tradition") Jewish doctrine or system of theosophy; tells the importance of humanity's role in God's Universe, and how an individual is the unfolding of God unto fullness; theory: the soul existed in a state of complete knowledge before reluctantly accepting a body.

Karma – (Sanskrit, Buddhism, Hinduism, Theosophy) the principle that makes every man or woman the cause of their present global location, lifestyle, relatives and physical body; law of action: for every action there is a reaction; karma works in one's favor or against one, doling out good or poor physical bodies and experiences; while living the results of the past, one is processing the condition of the future.

Kirlian photography – the process for taking pictures of the emanations and radiations surrounding objects and persons, which the human eye does not see; made possible by high voltage camera invented by Semyon and Valentina Kirlian, in Russia.

Laying-on-of-hands – to use one's hands to accelerate the normalizing of the patient's cells, so the patient's body can heal itself more quickly; the healer's hands are places over the congested area making physical contact or contacting a few inches above the body, or touching the head of the patient sending the bioenergy or magnetism to the diseased area.

Mantra – (Sanskrit) a significant sound which is psychically and scientifically known to affect human beings; used while meditating; sound can be a syllable, word, or a series of words or syllables; the sound is designed to assist one to attain higher states of consciousness, evoke Cosmic Energy to manifest within the meditator, dispel disease or create a blessing.

Mass hypnosis – to hypnotize the majority of people at lecture without them realizing that their level of awareness is altered; occurs, unconsciously or deliberately, if a leader is very impressive or charismatic or using deliberate techniques.

Quasi- – unreal; resembling but not being (the thing in question); to some degree; almost or somewhat. Latin *quasi,* contraction of *quansei* (unattested).

Quasiworld – a term for the genuine but invisible side of the Universe, which has existed forever and knows neither time nor space. It is the abode of the unconscious human mind and the source of paranormal phenomena.

Psi – (Heron) (the twenty-third letter of the Greek alphabet) arbitrarily chosen to represent an actual unknown quantity; a general term to identify a person's extrasensorimotor communication with the environment; currently popular to mean Psychic.

Spells – a word, words, music, or a chant designed to have a dominating or irresistible influence over another individual; to be under the control of another individual to a certain degree for a designated period of time.

Torah (Law) – the Five Books of Moses or the Torah of Moses. They are, in order, the books of Genesis, Exodus, Leviticus, Numbers, and Deuteronomy. The books based on revelations from God given to Israeli people.

BIBLIOGRAPHY

American Folk Medicine, University of California Press, Berkeley, California, 1976

Asher, Maxine. *Ancient Energy Key to the Universe*. Harper & Row, Publishers, Inc., N.Y., 1983

Avery, Jeanne. *A Soul's Journey*, Boru Books, Austin, Texas, 1996

Cranston, Sylvia. *Reincarnation. The Phoenix Fire Mystery*, Theosophical University Press, Pasadena, CA, 1994

Delys, Claudia. *A Treasury of Superstitions*, Gramercy Books, New York, 1997

Dossey, Larry, M.D. *Healing Words. The Power of Prayer and the Practice of Medicine*, HarperSanFrancisco, 1997

Dunne, Desmond. *Yoga. The Way to Long Life and Happiness*, Funk & Wagnalls, 1967

Gawain, Shakti. *Creative Visualization*, Bantam Books, New York, 1982

Gerber, Richard, M.D. *Vibrational Medicine: New Choices for Healing Ourselves*, Bear & Company, Santa Fe, New Mexico, 1987

Gerber, Richard, M.D. *A Practical Guide to Vibrational Medicine.Energy Healing and Spiritual Transformation,*Quill, New York, 2001

Greenbaum, Avraham. *The Wings of the Sun*, Breslow Research Institute, New York, 1995

Grig, E.R.N. *Biologic Reality*, Amaranth Books, Chicago, 1967

Grof, Stanisav. *The Adventure of Self-Discovery*, State University of New York Press, New York, 1988

Holzer, Hans. *Beyond Medicine*, Henry Regnery Company, Chicago, 1973

llich, Ivan. *Medical Nemesis*, Pantheon Books, New York, 1976

Irving, Oyle. *The Healing Mind*, Celestial Arts, Berkeley, California, 1975

Jarwis, D.C. *Folk Medicine*, Galahad Books, New York, 1996

Kaplan, Aryen. *Meditation and Kabbalah*, Samuel Weiser, York Beach, Maine, 1985

Kalweit, Holger. *Shamans, Healers, and Medicine*, Shambhala, Boston, 1992

Kastner, Mark & Burrough Hugh. *Alternative Healing*, Halcyon Publishing, La Mesa, 1994

Kenneth R. Pelletier. *Holistic Medicine: From Stress to Optimum Health*, Delacorte Press/Seymour Lawrence, 1979

Kersten, Holger, *Jesus lived in India*, Element, Rockport, Massaccuttes, 1994

Krueger, Victoria; Perrone, Bobette, and Stockel, H. Henrietta. *Medicine Women, Curanderas,and Women Doctors*, University of Oklahoma Press, 1989

Kunz, Dora (compiled). *Spiritual Aspects of the Healing Arts*, The Theosphical Publishing House, Wheaton, Illinois, 1985

Leadbeater, C.W. *The Chakras*, Theosophical Publishing House, London, 1975

LeShan, Lawrence. *How to Meditate*, Bantam Books, New York, 1975

Mails, Thomas E. *Fools Crow. Wisdom and Power*, Council Oak Books, Oklahoma, 1991

Mann, Felix. *Acupuncture. The Ancient Chinese Art of Healing and How it Works Scientifically*, Vintage Books, New York, 1973

Norman, C. Shealy. *Occult Medicine Can Save Your Life*, The Dial Press, New York, 1975

Niel, A. *Magic and Mystery in Tibet*, Dover, New York, 1971

Nielsen, Greg and Polansky, Joseph. *Pendulim Power*, Destiny Books, Rochester, Vermont, 1996

Palos, Stephan *The Chinese Art of Healing*, Herder and Herder, Inc., New York, USA, 1971

Siegel, Bernie S., M.D. *Love, Medicine & Miracles*, Harper & Row, Publishers, New York, 1990

Steiner, Rudolf by Querido, Rene. *A Western Approach to Reincarnation and Karma*, Anthroposophic Press, Hudson, New York, 1997

Агни Йога, С-Петербург, "Васильевский Остров", 1992

Васильев В., *Избранники Духов*, М. 1984

Традиционные и Естественные Методы Предупреждения и Лечения Рака, составитель Волосянко, М., Москва "Аквариум", 1994

Вронский С., *Астрономия, Суеверия или Наука*, М., 1990

Гримак Л., *Магия Биополя. Энергоинформационное Лечение*, Москва, Издательство "Республика", 1995

Давил- Неэл А., *Мистики и Маги Тибета,*Ростов-на-Дону, МП "Журналист", 1991

Давил- Неэл А., *Посвящения и Посвященные в Тибете*, Санкт-Петебург, "ОРИС", 1994

Донцов В., *Биоэнергетика Человека*, 1994

Ким, Л., *Опыт Исцеления. Школа Людмилы Ким*, "Молодая Гвардия", 1994

Мартынов А., *Неисповедимый Путь*, "Прометей", Москва, 1990

Мизун Ю., *Биопатогенные Зоны-Угроза Заболевания*, Москва, "Экология и Здоровье", 1993

Плужников А., *НЛО и Волшебные Рамки*, М. 1991

Повжитков А., Бойчук Р., *Основы Биоэнергетической Диагностики и Лечения*, М. 1991

Самолюк И., Лысеннюк В., Лимановский В., Лимановский Ю, и др. *Нетрадиционные Методы Диагностики и Терапия*, "Здоровье", Киев, 1994

Тибетская Книга Мертвых, "Двойная Звезда ", Москва, 1995

INDEX